Finding Jesus Christ

IN THE OLD TESTAMENT

Finding Jesus Christ in the Old Testament

All quoted scholars included in this book are members of The Church of Jesus Christ of Latter-day Saints. However, the contents of this book are not limited to members of The Church of Jesus Christ — it is meant for any and all who seek Jesus Christ. Please refer to https://www.churchofjesuschrist.org/ for Latter-day Saint doctrinal references and vocabulary explanations. Quotes have been modified for reader experience. Original transcripts can be found on https://followhim.co/.

© 2023 Follow Him Media Inc. All Rights Reserved.

All rights reserved. No portion of this book may be reproduced in any form without written permission from the publisher or author, except as permitted by U.S. copyright law.

ISBN 9798218186050

Excerpts from "Hold On, the Light Will Come", "Do I Make a Difference at All", and "Ninety and Nine" by Michael McLean.
Used by permission of Michael McLean.
© 1998 SHINING STAR MUSIC (ASCAP)

Book compilation by Annabelle Sorensen.
Cover design and book formatting by Alyssa Free.
Editing by Olivia N. Evans.

Visit the podcast website at https://followhim.co/.

This book was published using IngramSpark.
Printed in the U.S.A.

This book was inspired by the followHIM podcast, hosted by Hank Smith and John Bytheway.
FollowHIM was founded by Steve and Shan-
non Sorensen to be a resource for all to access
scholarly minds and their expertise in the gospel
of Jesus Christ. We now dedicate this book to
all those who strive to follow Jesus Christ and
seek to understand the mysteries of heaven. We
pray these truths will touch your heart, you will
feel the Holy Spirit testify to you of the reality
of a living God and your Savior Jesus Christ,
and you will feel inspired to find more of Jesus
Christ in your own daily life.

Contents

Contents

Genesis 1-3

Joshua Sears

> **Genesis 1:3** *And God said, Let there be light: and there was light.*

Science and religion are not pitted against each other.
Genesis isn't speaking the same language as
science; our cosmetology is not the same as
theirs. The Israelites didn't know what we know.
To them, the world was flat. To them, there
was water above and water below. Remember
when you're reading that they are speaking in
comparison to what they know, not to what
is science.

———

So what is God trying to say with Genesis? We
typically think it's to teach us how the earth was
created, but I don't think that is what God is
trying to do here. *I think He is trying to teach us who
He is, what His nature is, who people are, our relationship to each other, how we relate to God, and our purpose
here on earth.* And Genesis does that beautifully.

———

In ancient Israel, light was often used to represent a space where God is directly present. So now, God has created this environment *where He is directly present.*

———

That's what the creation is really teaching us, that *God prepared the earth for us. We are not an after-thought.* We are not just one of many creations, we are special in His sight. *We are fundamentally different from His other creations, as wonderful as they are.*

———

In ancient Israelite context, creating means you are bringing order to the chaos, so you structure things and give them purpose and meaning. That is why we can see Him taking our stories and our random events and granting us purpose and meaning. He can separate out the noise in our lives. "He can make something magnificent out of something unorganized." *God can give order to our chaos.*

———

We talked before about water being chaos. But yes, we see once it has its purpose and its function, *it becomes life-giving.*

———

God is very physically involved in creating the earth. He "formed" "bereaved" and "brought." It's kind of fun. He's down there in the mud making man, and just like He was physically involved then, *He is very physically involved in our lives now.*

———

One thing we can take away from the story of Adam and Eve is to see their story as an archetype for what we go through. By giving them names, it invites us to put ourselves in their shoes. They started in God's presence, they were taken out of God's presence, and we are trying to figure out how to get back to His presence. *Their story is all of our story.*

———

One of my favorite quotes from Joseph Smith is, All your losses will be made up to you in the resurrection provided you continue faithful. By the vision of the Almighty, I have seen it. In Joseph's words, that man knew loss, and he knew suffering, but he saw and knew perfectly *that every promised blessing could be ours, whether in this life or the next. So if you're going through one of those times right now, please do not give up. Trust that Heavenly Father will help you.* We have the testimonies of the prophets and the witnesses of people in the Bible who went before us that *God will not abandon us or forsake us. We'll have these Hezekiah, last-minute miracles come into our lives. And it might come later, it might come sooner. But Heavenly Father is someone we can trust.* We can have confidence in our trust in Him because He will never break trust with us. I want to share that testimony, in the name of Jesus Christ. Amen.

—

Genesis 3-4

Shon Hopkin

Genesis 3:6 *And when the woman saw that the tree was good for food, and that it was pleasant to the eyes, and a tree to be desired to make one wise, she took forth the fruit thereof, and did eat, and gave also unto her husband with her; and he did eat.*

There is a very significant difference in our modern worldview to the ancient worldview. *There isn't one viewpoint that is right and one that is wrong. God is God, God doesn't change.* The God we believe in is the same God they believe in, but it can be tricky, as we are reading words written by someone who lived in a very different time and a very different place, to not place our worldview onto *their worldview.*

———

Watery areas are a realm of chaos that humans don't really control. So when God creates the earth, He brings up order out of that chaos. It's like a watery birth. Just like a baby is born out of water, you get life that comes out of the chaos. So, God is going to bring order to all of that. *He brings life out of death. He brings life out of our chaos.*

———

I take the stories as literal as they are. These are real people with real lives, *but what I really care about is the why. What is going on? What is being communicated?* We take a very enlightened approach to our storytelling where there has to be an accuracy to the details, but ancient people often were more concerned about the accuracy of the message being conveyed.

———

The description of Eve is a "help meet." In Hebrew the word is *ezer kenegdo,* which means *a divine help who is his complimentary opposite, his equal.* God is setting up and showing us the power that comes when two people, *who are different, make a decision to come together and unite as one.*

———

I think there is some power in leaving the stories multivalent, meaning an ability for them to be seen or interpreted in different ways, from different angles, shedding new light at different times. *In our time, we like to dot the i's and cross the t's so we can stop thinking about it, but that is the power in not knowing — then we keep thinking.*

—

This is where the love story is enhanced. Eve has done something that is hurtful to her partner, and then she very powerfully and vulnerably stands in front of Adam and says, "I have eaten this fruit." Then Adam, with potential betrayal, looks at her and *he chooses* to see the woman that he loves, and *he decides, "We're in this together."* We now have a powerful example of a loving relationship. Like Eve, we can strive to be open and honest, and like Adam, we can strive to choose the team.

—

It is interesting that the concept of working for what we want — "I am going to earn my bread by the sweat of my brow" — is presented as one of the first laws of mortality. Our natural man is always looking for shortcuts. It is looking for ways to get something for nothing, to feel good without putting in the work. But because we are light and truth at our very core, this instinct to use sin as the shortcut warps who we are. *And that is why we need the redemption that comes through the Atonement of Jesus Christ — to remind us who we are, and that we, on our journey to become like the Savior Himself, are not meant to take the easy way.*

———

There is a Redeemer that turns this story back into gold. Even though Adam and Eve transgressed, even though *we* transgress, *we can return to live with God again. Because God loves us, He has provided a Savior of the world.*

———

This probably is the first place God teaches them the law of sacrifice. Think of the beauty of this sacrificial animal providing the skins, *the garments,* that are going to cover them as they leave the garden. *This sacrificial animal covers them. Christ covers them. God puts the image of the Atoning One on them to remind them who they are* — to remind them who they can become like. God is dressing them with power and protection as they leave the garden. *The skins serve as a reminder to them of their relationship with God, and that because of Jesus Christ, the Sacrificial Lamb, they can return back to the presence of God.*

———

There comes a moment when we are like, "it's not perfect," and there is a Fall, and then God is there to carry the story forward. We are not held captive by former mistakes, because God has offered us covenants just like He offered Moses, Noah, and Enoch.

—

I do not need to worry about my past because of the power of the Atonement of Jesus Christ. I do not need to worry about my future because of the power of covenants. *I know God is going to be there for me because He has promised He will be there for me.*

—

Digging deeper into the academic study of the Bible has only enhanced my understanding of the richness of what we are provided in the Restoration of the gospel. Where else are we living out these ancient stories? *They are alive, powerful, and applicable today.* We are making covenants. We're emphasizing covenants. We are listening to prophets. As Moses said, Would to God that all the Lord's people were prophets. I feel I've come to know God better as I've been guided toward him. *And as strange as it may sound to some listeners, the teachings of the Old Testament have helped me be a better man. There's a long way to go on that journey, but the Old Testament has only enhanced my relationships with others and the Lord.*

———

Genesis 5

Jenet Erickson

Genesis 5:1-2 *In the day that God created man, in the likeness of God made he him; Male and female created he them; and blessed them, and called their name Adam, in the day when they were created.*

Repentance is so difficult because of all the things Satan wants to distort. It is sin, repentance, the Atonement of Jesus Christ, and salvation. Repentance is often taught to be something to fear and avoid. *We even view repentance as punishment.* But what we have learned is that the Greek word for repentance is *metanoia*, meaning a change of mind, heart, and spirit, even breath. *When Jesus asks us to repent, it is all about growth, a change of mind and heart, and becoming, even healing — not penalty.*

—

This chapter shows us that we had to leave our Heavenly Parents so we could experience oppositional choices, so we could taste the bitter, so we could learn to prize the sweetness of what is good and pure. *That bitterness is sin, or weakness or transgression, and we taste it so we can know the sweet that is Christ*

—

When we see Christ as our Advocate in our personal life, not the Advocate *as in He takes the beating for us, but in our growth. That in our agony, He works in us and with us to overcome that — the shame, the fear, the weakness, and the predisposition to sin.* He heals that beautiful relationship as our Advocate.

—

The idea that we need to do it all right interferes with intimacy. It interferes with our relationships with ourselves and our children. *As long as we are hiding behind a false idea that there is some perfect way that we either should have been or should be, we have blocked intimacy.* The moment we can be honest in our fallibility to others and our children, when we are unafraid because we know Christ is our Advocate, they can trust us. Then we have given them the greatest gift: *to be comfortable in their fallibility, with Christ as their Advocate.*

—

This is the journey. *The moment we can turn and say, "I have failed you because I am a fallible person, and He is my Redeemer and He is yours."* Then we have entered into that space of a new level of intimacy.

———

That is what Adam starts with right here. We tear that mask off. *I need Christ, you need Christ. I am fallible, you are fallible. You are loved, I am loved, and His work is to help us grow and become.*

———

Agency is real. Cain made choices. And here is Adam, unafraid to say, "These are the problems in our family. *It is not something to hide from. It means there is the possibility of change."* Every family has real significant challenges, because that is the whole point: to learn and grow.

———

Parents, just like Adam and Eve, wrote their story through scripture. *Write your stories of repentance, of the Lord hearing your cry* and answering your prayers, helping you, and giving you strength.

—

There is power in identity. And that's why the Lord teaches it right here with Adam and Eve. Because knowing *I am a child of God, and you are a child of God, is the only absolutely secure and true identity we can have.*

—

The Lord never gives up. He keeps inviting His people to come back, turn, and repent.

—

I love that we get to read that God was angry. God is teaching us that anger has a rightful place. *All emotions and passions are given to us as gifts to teach us. Anger can lead us to see the truth of moral violations.* What we are to be careful of is when anger is coming from "me, me, me." *When it is no longer in service to other people, it is no longer in the bounds of the Lord.*

———

When we are honest about who we are, in our fallibility, and in our need for God, *He can be honest with us about who we can become.* But when we hide and fear our own weaknesses, we cannot hear Him say what we can become.

———

The Savior doesn't say, "your sins are not a big deal." He says, *"Come! Don't be afraid of your transgressions, I will heal you."*

———

Eating the fruit wasn't a mistake. Your mistakes are not a mistake. *Falling is THE plan so that we can use our agency to turn to Him to raise us up.* Agency is the very thing that enables us to become like Him.

———

Why does God spend *so much time talking about creation* and why did He give us so many beautiful, stunning, creations? Because He is reminding us, *"I am creating YOU."*

———

We have an epidemic of blame toward parents, and it's Satan. He's trying to tell people that, "You have no agency. You are locked into this." And that is not the path of repentance or healing for that child either. *When we are blaming another, we have given another power over our own journey with Christ. He is saying, "Come, this is all a journey for all of us, working together."* Forgiveness and compassion for parents is the way to healing as a person yourself.

———

I think I came into motherhood with the list of
things I was going to do, and these little people
were going to just go right along with what I
wanted and my working out their salvation. I
knew all the right things. Then I realized my
perfectionism blocked my experience of my
children and our experience of Christ together.
This is not me having them experience Christ
my way, it is us experiencing the redemption
of Christ together. My efforts to have my kids
feel and experience the gifts of the Holy Ghost
through my own repentant heart and their
experiencing that vulnerability and openness
from me, just learning that instead of my list of
things that I'm going to do and make happen
has been such a journey of growth. So, I'm
so thankful for the Redeemer. This is what it's
taught me: I need him. We need him

—

Genesis 6-11

Krystal Pierce

Genesis 8:1 *And God remembered Noah, and every living thing, and all the cattle that was with him in the ark: and God made a wind to pass over the earth assuaged;*

Science is sometimes used as a weapon against religion, and that blows my mind. *God invented science. God is science. It's okay that sometimes things don't make sense.* We don't know the logistics of the Flood or the logistics of other stories, and that's okay. Not having a full understanding doesn't make it not true or wrong.

———

In the Old Testament, we get caught up in the what and the how. Like sacrificing animals — it's hard for us to connect to this because we don't do this anymore. But when we think about the why, which is to show our love to God, to receive blessings, and to give thanks, we quickly can see that we do sacrifice for those things — the how just looks different.

———

You don't have to earn God's love. You don't need to build a tower to get to Him. *All you need to do is open your eyes to how He is already there.*

———

As we have gone through Genesis, we have experienced some major falls and comebacks. *Remember the comeback. Some people survive this. Noah's family survives this, Jared's family survives this, so how do we? When we experience our falls, our towers, our Floods, how do we survive?* You *can* survive. *It is with the help of God they survive.*

———

The story of the sons of God and the daughters of God is teaching us that *people influence each other.* People have an effect on each other. Who you are around, and who you speak to, affect your life. *This story is a warning that in the same way righteousness can spread from individual to individual, wickedness can spread, too.*

———

Sometimes we feel like a grasshopper, and we're fighting against giants. And they have the power, the control, and maybe the wealth and the status. And we feel like we can't. But we read here, "Noah had the power of God with him." *We also can have the power of God with us. You might feel like a grasshopper, but God can make you a giant.* Just like David had the power of God with him and was able to fight and beat his giant, you can beat yours.

—

Even though Noah is surrounded by wickedness and the rulers are trying to kill him, and he is losing friends to wickedness, *he still stays faithful. And I think THAT is what we are supposed to take out of the story — that WE can stay faithful.*

—

Noah listened, he obeyed, and he prepared. Noah didn't get an easy out here. He is literally asked to build an ark. *Sometimes God stops trials, but more often than not God says, "Here is something you can do to survive the trial," and that is mercy, too."*

———

The Lord gave Noah all of the information, everything he needed to be ready for when the Flood came — *spiritual and temporal. We can liken this to our own work to prepare for our floods. In what way has the Lord or the prophet prepared us for upcoming trials in our own life?* How do we prepare both *physically* and *spiritually* so that when the flood comes we will make it through?

———

This is the message of the Flood: *Be ready, and be prepared for when the Savior comes again.*

———

The whole point of a chiasmus is to say to us, "This is the moral of the story." And the first verse in chapter 8 says, *"God remembered Noah."* *This* is what we are supposed to focus on. I love that God remembers them. The subsiding of the wind happens *in the middle of the Flood — in the middle of the trial.* When we are in the middle of our trials, God remembers us. He does not say, "Good luck, see you on the other side." He is there the whole time. *He remembers Noah. He remembers you.*

———

The same thing that was said to Adam and Eve was said to the people on the ark when they left the ark: "Go and replenish the earth." So it's symbolic of this renewal, a fresh start, and a cleansing that has happened. And *that* is what the Flood represents. *This is mercy — that everyday we can repent, that we can become cleansed, and that we can become someone new.*

———

What I know for sure about my Heavenly Father and how much he loves me, is He sent his Son, and that Jesus is the Christ that went through the Atonement and the Crucifixion, and that's what matters — *that's what matters.* If I can go back to that and I can build on that, then I'll never get lost. I love that I use my studies in the classroom to talk about God. I love that I can talk about archeology and faith in the exact same sentence. These are things that I love. And I know these things come from God. And that keeps me grounded, I think, being okay with who I am — that I have all these different parts of my identity, including being a professor, being a mom, being a spouse, and I try to balance these things and make sense out of them.

———

Genesis 12-17

Jennifer C. Lane

> **Genesis 17:7** *And I will establish my covenant between me and thee and thy seed after thee in their generations for an everlasting covenant, to be a God unto thee, and to thy seed after thee.*

In the ancient Near East, people would become slaves or be in bondage, and we see that language in scripture a lot. But people could be bought out of bondage by a payment of a price, and that's such a powerful gospel concept — that *Christ pays a price for us to bring us out of bondage.* We can have confidence that, as our Kinsman Redeemer, *He will come to get us. He will buy us out of bondage.*

———

When we put our trust in Him and don't worry about ourselves, then we can have the confidence that we can do whatever He asks us to do. *Because it's not about us,* it's not about our capacity. *It's about His capacity,* and that's infinite.

———

"Fear not Abraham, I am thy shield and thy great reward." So what is it we get from serving the Lord? *He is giving us Himself.*

———

She trusted the Lord, *and the Lord's promise is more powerful than nature.*

—

The Lord won't change our heart without our permission, because we are agents. But when we want it, and we start to ask for it, He can help us. *He will start to change it.*

—

Even though we go through years, maybe even decades, of not understanding, that's where faith comes in — in trusting the Lord to keep going, *to trust that His promises are sure.* We don't necessarily know when they are going to be fulfilled or how they are going to be fulfilled, *but we don't have to know that, because we know Him.* We know He loves us, and that can bring us comfort and peace when we don't have answers.

—

I think that's what the Lord expects of us, *just to keep going.*

———

Trust that holiness is happiness. Trust that following the Lord's way is the path of happiness. *That takes faith.*

———

Abraham has set the model for how to walk away from the world and how to walk toward God.

———

Whatever we spend time with is going to change us.

———

When you know through personal experience these things are true, *it doesn't mean you have answers to everything.* I found that I know what matters: getting on the path, staying on the path, and keeping the relationship with the Lord. I don't have the answers, but I know the Lord loves me. And I know that His promises are sure, and so I don't have to. The prophets don't have to have done everything right or said everything right, because they're human beings. So, my confidence isn't in them; my confidence is in the Lord, Jesus Christ. And He's working with them. He's working with me. As long as we are true to Him and the covenants we've made, He'll get us there. So that's what I've come to know, and everything I study deepens my conviction that that's real and deepens my appreciation for the privilege of being part of His work.

—

Genesis 18-23

Daniel C. Peterson

> **Genesis 21:6** *And Sarah said, God hath made me to laugh, so that all that hear will laugh with me.*

When the Lord says, "Get out", *Get out! The Lord means now!* The longer you hang around, the more likely you are going to start taking on the coloration of your environment.

—

Like Lot's wife, it is easy to feel comfortable where we are. It is easy to think the past is greater than the future, *but it's not. The future is what holds possibility. The future is what God is preparing us for.*

—

We should not be reading this and saying, "this is just like Bob." Rather, we should be saying, *"Lord is it I? Am I the one who is guilty of this?"* And the answer all too often is yes. Those have been the greatest moments in scripture for me, when I realize, *"this is me."* I can't point fingers. *Who am I to judge?*

—

This is THE Abrahamic test — total submission to the Lord's will. Isaac trusts God and he trusts his father.

—

Sometimes it is not about the problem itself; it is about us learning how to deal with the problem or what we are capable of.

—

The gospel of Jesus Christ laid out the Plan of Salvation in a way that I had never heard before. I don't know, just the whole sweep of the thing from premortal existence through immortal life, life afterward, and the potential destiny of human beings. I just thought, "this is the grandest, most spectacular thing I have ever read in my life." And so to me, early on, there was a sense of the grandeur of the vision of the gospel and the intellectual excitement of it that has never left me. I still feel that this is the grandest vision, the greatest story that I can imagine. There's just nothing better.

———

Genesis 24-27

Camille F. Olson

Genesis 26:24 *I am the God of Abraham thy father: fear not, for I am with thee, and will bless thee, and multiply thy seed for my servant Abraham's sake.*

You cannot tell the story and *do not see* the story of God's people anywhere without seeing women very prominently.

—

The Old Testament shows the humanness of these individuals. *You cannot confuse the character of the Lord with any of the other characters.* He stands out. They are imperfect people trying to do the best they can. And the Lord empowers them to do beyond their natural ability even when they continue to stumble and fall, *and that ought to be very encouraging to us.*

—

We can get so caught up in stories and personalities of the Bible that we forget the purpose of these stories is to bring us to Jesus Christ. *They are here to help us find Him.*

—

These stories collectively and individually *show us that we are stronger when we work together* — men and women working together, using the talents and inspiration that God gives each one of us.

—

Every time it says *"the way"*, I put Christ there, *because Christ is the way.* I think you see that in these stories. It reminds you to look at your own life, and you see He has been there to *show us* the way as well.

—

They asked Rebekah, and she said, *"I will go."* She is not coming back, she is giving her life for this family. *We are all asked to do challenging things,* and these women, like Rebekah, can be our examples.

—

Rebekah does not hesitate. She's not hoping the commandment changes by the time she gets there, *she's acting.* I look at Rebekah and ask myself, "how do *I* respond when God gives *me* direction?"

—

In every single case of those times of emptiness, that's when each of these women cement a relationship with God. Sometimes when blessings don't come in the way you expect *or when you* expect, and you are an outlier in any way, and you go to church and maybe church doesn't quite connect with what you are going through because it assumes you are like everybody else, that's when you start seeing. *God is aware of you. I think of Hagar saying, "a god who sees me."*

—

The Lord is not deceived here. *The Lord is never deceived.*

—

The Bible tells us that the Lord's plan for this family, *and every family, is one of redemption.*

———

Rebekah is communicating with the Lord and gets an answer that is clear, precise, detailed, and informative. That indicates to me *that prayer is not an anomaly for Rebekah. She knows the Lord, and she knows His voice.* We don't have those verses, but if you read between the lines, *she has been pouring out her heart.*

———

This is such a real story. *It's messy, just like our lives.* Nobody has a perfect life or a perfect family; *we all need a Redeemer.*

———

Whatever station we are in, whatever our circumstances, when we have an opportunity to help we should be willing to step forward, whether it is feeding one hundred prophets in caves or giving the very last out of our cupboard. So it's in those extremities that we discover Him and that we are not to be afraid of what He desires to show us with a still, small voice. I think that's a compliment when we can hear and understand a still, small voice versus having lightning coming out of heaven. Do not get discouraged if there are times of quietness when it seems like nothing is happening. It's sometimes in those quiet times that we learn things that we could never know if we are feeling a more intense relationship with the Lord.

—

Genesis 28-33

Jeffrey Chadwick

Genesis 28:12 *And he dreamed, and behold a ladder set up on the earth, and the top of it reached to heaven: and behold the angels of God ascending and descending on it.*

Jacob was not expecting a dream or revelation, and that's important because it teaches us that *the Lord will be in places you don't expect.*

———

You see some tension between Isaac and Rebekah, you see some tension between Sarah and Abraham, and Jacob and Rachel, etc. *You see everything we go through.* It's amazing if you understand the context of scripture and also the covenant and belief that they have how *they make it work in spite of all the problems.*

———

This is why we have to leave the ultimate judgment in the hands of the Lord, because there are a lot of good people who aren't living their life the way you are.

———

If you will do everything you can to overcome a perceived hurt from someone, then you let things work out, very often, *the goodness of people comes out.*

—

I bear two witnesses to all my students about our scriptures, and particularly the ancient scriptures that I deal more with because of where I'm at and what I do. I bear witness that they are true. That's a spiritual statement. I bear witness also that they are authentic, that they are what they claim to be. I especially drive that home because the Bible's very complicated, but the Book of Mormon and how we got it today is simple. It was given to the prophet Joseph Smith by an angel who translated it by the gift and power of God, and it is a translation of real things that happened to real people in real ancient times.

—

Genesis 37-41

Lili De Hoyos Anderson

> **Genesis 39:2** *And the Lord was with Joseph, and he was a prosperous man; and he was in the house of his master the Egyptian.*

We can speculate how things happened, but *Genesis covers more than 2,000 years of history.* I want people to appreciate that if there are things they feel are not fully fleshed out, well, that's right. This is a pretty brief record of these marvelous events. Nevertheless, we have this record preserved so we can learn from these amazing believers who lived at the beginnings of the world. *So, just be patient as we read this book.*

—

When I started reading the Bible again this year, I was thinking how impressive it is that these people, *on their own, without much support, decide to be believers and followers of God.* It made me recognize what a great blessing it is to live in a dispensation where there are so many believers we can connect with so easily worldwide.

—

None of us get perfect parents and none of us are perfect parents, and that is the plan. However, that is not a free pass to be a lousy parent. We are asked by God to be diligent in being a good parent, and as we strive to be a better parent, *that is when Christ will help turn us into a better person.*

——

God's *not* kidding around that there are tests in life. Are we aware of what an Abrahamic test really is? It gets us right in our hang-ups, *the things that God knows we can overcome. He wants to make our weaknesses strong.*

——

The sweet spot is not expecting ourselves to be perfect whilst not condoning sin and throwing out the rules, and saying, "Because life is hard, it doesn't matter if you're good." Yes it does! *It absolutely matters! That is the point.* Can we, through all the tribulation of this life, continue to choose Christ and come unto Him and be saved?

——

God works through everybody, *righteous and unrighteous.* He uses Joseph's brothers to accomplish an amazing salvation of Israel. *The Lord will use our behaviors, good or bad, to accomplish His purposes.* But *there will be* accountability for people who sin.

——

If it were easy, everybody would get better. But it's a journey, and the Healer is Christ. *So don't give up. Hold onto this hope in Christ that is hope for a glorious resurrection, but also hope that our wounds will be healed.*

——

It's beautiful when Joseph says, "The Lord giveth and the Lord taketh away, *blessed be* the name of the Lord." *That can be me, and that can be you. We can be those people.* We can thank the Lord, even when life is not fair.

——

This is super important to understand: *It is not a mistake that hard things happen, it is the plan.* God set up the world to be a big spiritual weight room. Just like physical muscle, we can't build spiritual muscle without doing some resistance training — *without lifting some weight.* And that is what hard things do to our spiritual muscles, *they give us an opportunity to strengthen them. We are meant to become stronger. God knows how strong we can become.*

———

Life has to be unfair, otherwise it would have no meaning. *We would not be challenged. We would not be changed.*

———

We cannot fool God. All things are known to Him.

———

We are here to grow, and we are here to become like the Savior Himself. Where do we think that is going to happen? At the spa? *That is why life is unfair, because that is what will give us the opportunity to become like Him.*

———

It says *"and the Lord was with Joseph."* God is not *with Joseph* because He likes him better than the others, God doesn't do that. He is "no respecter of persons." So why, then, was the Lord with Joseph? *The only answer is because Joseph was with the Lord. Joseph chose the Lord again and again.* He keeps choosing God after all his unjust circumstances and trials and difficulties. *He uses his agency every time to choose Him.* And when we choose God, even in *our* trials and difficulties, we receive this amazing blessing, too: *God will be with us.*

———

Joseph is not looking for trouble, trouble comes to him and he resists temptation. *He fled.* Sometimes it's important to leave and get back on holy ground.

———

It's amazing what God can do with us. He can even take me and turn me into something divine. And when I am choosing Him, I don't doubt that He is there with me, even when I don't feel it in the immediate sense.

———

It's *our choice* to let God consecrate our afflictions *for our good* or to be miserable.

———

Don't be deceived. There are so many blessings that God gives us because of the affliction and suffering. He tells us we *will know* the bitter. But *if we do not become bitter,* and *we keep choosing Him,* we don't even know how good it is going to be. It is going to be tremendous.

———

So much suffering is wasted. There is *always* something to learn in our trials.

———

We are *never* abandoned when we choose God. *He will be with us.*

———

The point of education is to realize how much
we don't know and that we should be seekers
of truth. Here we have a god, willing to share
truth. He puts it in scripture and He gives us
the Spirit. Don't doubt. Pray more. Ponder
more. Seek more. If we think we're already
full of light and truth without Him, how silly is
that? Where do we think our good ideas come
from in the first place? All our good ideas came
from Him. We lose out if we don't use Christ
as our North and the scriptures as our guide. It
protects us from the wiles of the Adversary. It
protects us from deception. It protects us from
falsehoods. What a great gift we can give our
children if we can teach them this humility and
gratitude for the light and truth that God wants
to give us.

———

Genesis 42-50

S. Michael Wilcox

> **Genesis 43:30** *And Joseph made haste; for his bowels did yearn upon his brother: and he sought where to weep; and he entered into his chamber, and wept there.*

If I had to say, "what does the story of Joseph teach us?" or Ruth, or Jonathan, or dozens of others, it would be that you and I get *vivid* pictures of *purity and spiritual triumph.* We get a definitive view of what *true goodness is.*

—

Genesis is the very first book of scripture God gives us, the first book that anybody is going to read. It's the book that has been around the longest, so it is safe to assume that it is going to have some of the most critical lessons for the human experience. If somebody asked me, "Can you recommend a good book on how to have good family relationships?" I'd say, "Oh sure, read Genesis with that question in mind, and look at all the relationships." *This is God's first message He wants us to understand, the family.* He doesn't show us perfect families; these families have challenges, that's part of the beauty of it. *But out of them you get spiritual triumphs.*

—

The first great message of Joseph's life is given before he is even born, when Laban creates the first family dysfunction. It is a lesson for all of us who are thinking, "It's my life, I can do what I want," who think in the more immediate now instead of the long term. So I say to all of us, including myself, *think of the long-term impact on others those decisions are going to have, especially those who are not born.*

———

Joseph teaches us *if you find yourself living an unexpected life, make the best of it, and don't get mad at God.*

———

The second great truth that Joseph teaches us is that *God can turn all negatives into positives and can make us fruitful in the "land of our afflictions."*

———

The third great truth of Joseph is that *things that appear to be against you may in reality be blessings. They may be, for you, the opposite of what you perceive.*

———

One of the great themes throughout all of Genesis is when someone sins against you, or when someone hurts you, *forgive them, especially* if they are members of your family.

———

Four of the most beautiful words in Genesis are when Joseph says to his brothers, *"come near to me,"* and then "they came near." *If possible,* invite or initiate the "coming near." *It's not just forgiveness, it's a reconciliation — a restructuring of a relationship that has been damaged or wounded.*

———

I wonder how often God weeps when we don't really believe He forgives us. When He says, "Look, *I have not only forgiven, I forget.*" And it is important in our relationship to realize that He not only forgives, but there is forgetfulness in the relationship, and we need to forget it too. So, when forgiveness is offered to you freely from another, *accept it* and *find the forgetfulness in it.*

———

No matter what people do to hurt you, no matter what happens, if you stay on the path, *God will make it good.* Life is fair, life is just — or at least *eternity is.* And it is going to be that way because God has the power and ability to make it that way. This is the plan of happiness and He wants us to be happy, and that's how it is going to end.

———

Our interpretation of events, and even proph-ecies, may change *dramatically* with time and perspective.

———

I was blessed with a believing heart. It's a
good thing, because I also have a questioning
mind. Sometimes the believing heart and the
questioning mind have some interesting con-
versations with each other. So occasionally,
my mind has to tell my heart, We need to look
at this with reason. And sometimes my heart
has to say to my mind, You have to trust me. I
have wrestled with just about every issue in the
Church. I have learned to live with imperfect
scriptures, imperfect people, imperfect prophets, imperfect me, and imperfect organizations.
Sometimes faith is like a tiny, tiny little ledge on
a high mountain cliff. I haven't been walking on
a tiny ledge all my life, but I know what it's like
to walk on a tiny ledge and have the road widen
and go back, and it goes back to a tiny ledge.
So, we hold on.

———

Exodus 1-6

Anthony Rivera Jr.

Exodus 3:10-11 *Come now therefore, and I will send thee unto Pharaoh, that thou mayest bring forth my people the children of Israel out of Egypt. And Moses said unto God, Who am I, that I should go unto Pharaoh, and that I should bring forth the children of Israel out of Egypt?*

We're going to see Moses as a representative of us, *of one who is working out his salvation.* I think we can relate to his humble upbringing, to cultural impacts, to being alone in the desert, meeting a mentor, having some sort of fatherly figure, marriage, family, meeting God, getting close to Him, asking questions, and *going on various life missions in the service of God.*

—

Sometimes we come from backgrounds of families that have to make difficult decisions and that are living in times that are challeng-ing. Sometimes we feel like we are being sent down the Nile, and we can't steer and we end up somewhere, and we grow up in a culture that may not be telling us exactly who we are, so *something needs to happen. Something needs to happen where we can be led to this discovery of who we really are.*

—

God knows the plan and He does these preparations, but sometimes it takes time to get us into the position where we are ready to engage them to discover why and what we need to do.

—

Our God is a *personal* God.

—

Let me tell you this: the Lord is hastening His work. He's working on these people. And I hope that members feel that same spirit as they study this incredible scripture, because, like we saw today, the Spirit is there. We need to remember God keeps reminding Moses to remind Israel about Abraham, and Isaac, and Jacob. He's intertwining in the text to remember the Creation, to remember the Garden. And we see it written throughout all scripture from the Book of Mormon, which understands it completely and gets it, to modern-day revelation.

—

Exodus 7-13

Andrew C. Skinner

Exodus 12:13 *And the blood shall be to you for a token upon the houses where ye are: and when I see the blood, I will pass over you, and the plague shall not be upon you to destroy you, when I smite the land of Egypt.*

Exodus 7–13 is a foundational, if not *the foundational,* story of deliverance in the Old Testament. It's *the prototypical story for divine deliverance.* It serves as the foundation for the kind of deliverance that *we receive* from the Atonement of the Lord Jesus Christ.

———

Genesis is family history. So we can't forget *we are talking about us here. We are part of this family.* We ourselves are part of this Israelite community. *This is our story.*

———

The human family's first testament of Jesus Christ *is* the Old Testament.

———

The Lord loves all of His children, *and He will not go back on His promises.*

———

There are all kinds of bondages that people grow under in our day. We are so grateful then that we have this model that *reassures us that Jehovah, in ancient times, had enough power to bring about His purposes. Jesus Christ, in our day, has enough power to bring about His purposes.* And if we extend that, the real lesson is *Jesus Christ and our Father in Heaven have enough power to answer our prayers,* no matter what our challenges.

———

Faith in the Lord Jesus Christ means that you trust that He has enough power to bring about His purposes *using you. In you, He will manifest His powers.*

———

Jesus Christ is *the* greatest manifestation of Heavenly Father's love for us. That takes us to the central characteristic of God. 1 John 4: God is love. *Everything that God does is influenced and shaped and mediated by His perfect love. That is the essence of His personality.*

———

Interestingly enough, by the Lord asking us to offer a broken heart and contrite spirit, He is asking us to offer the very things that Jesus Himself offered. In Gethsemane, His spirit was crushed — that's the meaning of the word contrite. So, that happens in Gethsemane to the Savior. How did He die on the cross? In his book "Jesus the Christ", Elder Talmage says that He died from *a broken heart, or a ruptured heart. So, the very things that Jesus Himself offered as part of His Atonement are now the things that we must offer after the shedding of His blood.* We must offer our broken heart and contrite spirit. *We must, in a sense, relive Gethsemane and Golgotha in our own lives.*

———

God guides us away from things that we may not be able to handle. And if we listen to Him, then we can enjoy His blessings. *And if we don't listen, then we have no promise.*

———

I cannot remember a time when I didn't know these things were true. I wish I could say, Oh, I had this dramatic conversion experience, but I'm one who didn't. *One of the key elements in my faith trajectory has been a deeper appreciation of Jesus Christ's centrality in everything, and also our Heavenly Father's interest in each one of us.* I don't pretend to know how our Heavenly Father and His Son can know each of us so intimately and so well; I know that they do, and that's been a source of strength. It's gotten us through some recent hard times. Now you understand what He felt in the Garden and on the cross. This has been a significant period of growth for me, even this late in my life.

———

Exodus 14-17

Matthew L. Bowen

> **Exodus 14:14** *The Lord shall fight for you, and ye shall hold your peace.*

We shouldn't be looking at the Israelites thinking, "Dumb Israelites." We should be saying to ourselves, "How am I like this?" We will start to realize we are a lot more like them than we think.

———

It can seem so counterintuitive, the moves that the Lord guides us to make sometimes. We feel like it is an inspired decision at the time, and then when we go forward and act on it we find ourselves thinking that it seems like things aren't working out or aren't going the way they should go. That's when we get to remember that the Lord… *He has the strategy.* Sometimes we need to step away from our perspective and *step into God's eye view.*

———

The Lord is the ultimate chess master, and He is thinking, *"There is nothing your agency can do that My accounting cannot account for."*

———

Sometimes we see death as a great finale to a one act play, when really there is a three act play going on and the first and third acts are of much greater length than any of us imagine. *The first one had no beginning and the third one no end, and yet the second is so determinative in the trajectory of where the third act goes.*

———

The Lord will fulfill His covenants. He fulfilled them for Abraham and Isaac and Jacob; *He will fulfill them for us too.* God keeps every promise to us in time and eternity. *So, if there is anything we feel like the Lord has deprived us of in mortality, it is going to be done to us.*

———

We *never* get to the point, as students of the scriptures, where we will have exhausted our capacity to learn more, to understand them with a greater depth, or to be drawn closer to Christ.

———

When we remember Christ and we covenant our willingness to remember Him, we're not just remembering Him and His atoning sacrifice, *we are also remembering all the other acts of deliverance great and small — all the other miracles in our lives that He is providing.*

—

The Lord is not expecting perfection from us, so we should not expect instant gratification of our desires from Him.

—

The journey is not easy, *but the Lord provides.*

—

I know that it is all in His hands. Our time here will not be that long, but I think we will be grateful for all the relationships we've developed. The Lord's goodness has manifested to me in wonderful ways. And I couldn't have done anything that I've done without the help of a lot of people helping me and shaping me and empowering me. I would close with a testimony of Jesus, knowing He lives. And I know that He atoned for me, that He atoned for all humankind, and that He is the Way, the Truth, and the Life. He can show us the way because He is the Way that the Atonement is real. And one day we'll know it even better than we know now, and the proof will be unmistakable. We will then realize how much we love Him and how much He loves us.

—

Easter

Bruce C. Hafen and
Marie K. Hafen

> ***Isaiah 53:4*** *Surely he hath borne our griefs, and carried our sorrows: yet we did esteem him stricken, smitten of God, and afflicted.*

In a sense, the story of the life of Christ is the story of *giving* the Atonement. The story of Adam and Eve is the story of *receiving* the Atonement. *That is us. We are Adam and Eve.*

—

The Atonement of Jesus Christ *is not just about erasing black marks,* it's developmental. Because of the Atonement of Christ, we can learn from our experience *without being condemned by it.*

—

Sometimes we have to act without knowing exactly how things are going to work out, relying solely on faith in Christ and His mission.

—

We have to *be like Him to be able to recognize Him.* So if you can see Him in your life now, you can know you will recognize Him when He comes later.

—

Elder Hafen: Some people sometimes ask, "So, we're not supposed to doubt? That's wrong?" Elder Maxwell wrote a letter to one of his grandkids that had asked him about doubt, and he said, Doubting can either strengthen or weaken our faith, depending on our supply of meekness. Sounds like Elder Maxwell, doesn't it? And so if we're not meek, then all the other tools for dealing with questions and problems will not be very helpful.

——

Sister Hafen: Questions and doubts could be really good.

——

Elder Hafen: If you can be meek about it, it can open the door to a whole gospel subject

——

Exodus 18-20

Daniel L. Belnap

> **Exodus 20:20** *And Moses said unto the people, Fear not: for God is come to prove you, and that his fear may be before your faces, that ye sin not.*

The more things that need to be spelled out to us, the less we have in our own spiritual growth. Ultimately, *we* are responsible for *our own* spiritual welfare.

—

Do we think about what it's like to be in the presence of God? Do we imagine what eternal life is like? *Imagination plays a fundamental role in the expression of faith* — looking forward with an eye of faith and seeing something that hasn't been yet, *but will be.* That ability to look up, or as Peter says, "see afar off," becomes *essential* to survival.

—

When you are engaged in true gratitude, *it becomes revelatory. It reveals to you what has been done* and in particular the way in which the Lord has been involved in your life, which gives you the power and the strength to move forward into the future with that trust.

—

We are sustained by God's faith *in us and* our faith *in God.*

—

We define faith too often as an engagement where we lack knowledge, so it's "I don't know, therefore I have to have faith." But in this case — and in most scriptural examples dealing with faith — faith is reliant on *what you do know, and the more you know, the more faith you have.* That connection to knowledge is something we don't often think about but is vital to faith. *Your faith is stronger the more you know, the more you understand and see the Lord's hand in your life.*

—

We may be the offspring of God, but what makes Him our Father is His ability to bless us. *And what makes us His sons and daughters is our choosing to receive.*

—

Why would He give you the commandment if He didn't actually think you could pull it off? When God says, "Be ye therefore perfect," I think, "Oh, so it's achievable. *It's doable." Even if it's a process, do not be dismayed by the promise itself. God would not give it if He did not think you could pull it off.*

———

From an eternal perspective, from *His view, I don't think He sees as much space between us as we like to think that there is.* It's a perspective, and He has an eternal one. I don't, so by virtue of that, as I look at these laws, they are not for children; *they are for adults.* He is saying, *"If I am going to take this seriously, I expect you to take this seriously too."*

———

I believe in the importance of seeing afar off
to have this cosmic perspective of reality. I
think that changes everything. I believe it has
the potential to bring about that great gift that
Christ promises, which is peace. And He talks
about peace in John: This peace I've given
to you, that's not like the world, but a divine
peace. So that peace comes from that bigger
perspective, and that bigger perspective is more
enhanced the more windows that you have. If
all you've got is a biblical text, and if all you've
got are academic methodologies, they limit the
view. They're limited to this time and space,
and a very limited aspect of this particular time
in space. But the restored scriptures and the
Old and New Testament expand that horizon.
They expand the context and the contours of
these things.

———

Exodus 24, 31-34

John Hilton III

> **Exodus 25:8** *And let them make me a sanctuary; that I may dwell among them.*

For any of us who might feel like, "Oh, does anyone know what we're doing?" *Probably not,* but *it is* making a big difference.

——

Sometimes you might not have a certain talent. Maybe you feel like, "Well the spirit hasn't filled me with a talent of art, so I'm not going to be able to contribute." I love how the verse actually says "every one whose heart stirred him up" to come unto the work to do it was called. *You don't have to have mad skills. The Holy Ghost will bless you when you stand up and start working. Your talents will be magnified.*

——

You might feel like you don't have the natural capabilities. *But when you are called to the work, the Lord can magnify whatever you have.* And sometimes a call is a self-call, where you feel inspired to go and contribute.

——

The Sabbath is not a day of don'ts, it is a day of do's. There are so many good things that we can do. If we have in our hearts the principle of healing, glorifying God, and asking what sign we are sending, the Spirit will guide us.

—

God has all power, and He can heal us. But sometimes for His wisdom, *He will delay.* If you are in the delay, I testify to you that Jesus Christ lives. *Do not lose hope. Keep going strong.* As you work through the delay, the healing will come. Someday, it might be today, it might not be to-morrow, and it might not be until the next life, *but healing will come. Stay close to Jesus, because He is real. And He is the source of that healing.*

—

I have never desired a golden calf in my life, but I think about what that might represent in my life. Maybe we are thinking Jesus plus a good job, or Jesus plus a good marriage. But *I think this is a reminder that Jesus is enough, period. Am I looking for my security in something other than the Savior?* Because if I am, I am going to come up short and feel pain. Because other things will fail me at one time or another.

———

I love that the Lord says, "I know you, by name." It gives us a sense of the type of relationship we can have with the Lord. *He knows us by name and cares about us.* So when we put that extra time and effort in to develop a relationship with Him, that *is not time wasted.*

———

God wants to make something *amazing* out of us. And He is wanting us to connect with Him, not for His own purpose, *but so that He can make more of us than we can make of ourselves.*

———

In so many ways the story of Exodus, and Moses in particular, is the story of Jesus. And that is true with every other passage of scripture. We see the story of David and Goliath is about someone who is weak, defeating the strong — for us, *Jesus. We can find Jesus in all of these Old Testament passages.*

———

Things did work out in the long run. Eventually, I was able to get a Ph.D. I got hired for my dream job. Looking back, I feel like this whole episode was part of the Lord doing a remarkable thing in my life, but that doesn't mean it wasn't painful at the time. And going back to one of the principles we discussed earlier — the golden calf. I think for me, my golden calf knew exactly how everything was going to work out. That's still one of the idols that I have today. I don't like uncertainty. I don't like surprises. And in this case, I didn't know how things were going to happen, and it was so painful. So I was saying, Yes, Jesus is enough. But really, what I meant was Jesus plus knowing everything's going to work out, that's enough — and being able to see every detail.

———

Exodus 35-40, Leviticus 1; 16; 19

Matthew Grey

> ***Exodus 36:3*** *And they received of Moses all the offering, which the children of Israel had brought for the work of the service of the sanctuary, to make it withal. And they brought yet unto him free offerings every morning.*

I like to think of temple preparation as learning a language. We need to learn the language of ritual and symbolism and the type of things we would encounter in a temple space. Because if it's like learning a normal language, *it means that we need to pay a certain price to learn the vocabulary. And when we pay that price to learn that language, and then go to that space, what was once a very frustrating and confusing experience can become a very communicative experience.* Now you not only know what is going on, but it is *meaningful* to you. *It is revealing things to you, whereas before it felt like things were being concealed from you.*

———

The process of scholarship can include a lot of wrestling. I think those are necessary moments. I don't think that becoming a disciple scholar comes easily or cheaply. It comes through a lot of soul-searching and a lot of needing to process new information. So, I have come to realize, "Oh, the biblical text is more complicated than I once thought." Or, "Maybe these authorship issues are a little more nuanced than I once thought." And I think that that is exactly the type of process that we need to go through to be effective teachers in the Church and teachers in God's kingdom — to have an informed faith, an informed discipleship. None of us are finished products and we're still in process, but I have thoroughly been enriched by the challenges of combining faith and scholarship.

—

Numbers
11-14, 20-24

Kerry Muhlestein

> ***Numbers 14:18*** *The Lord is longsuffering, and of great mercy, forgiving iniquity and transgression, and by no means clearing the guilty, visiting the iniquity of the fathers upon the children unto the third and fourth generation.*

Since the Bible is Israel's family history, that means it is *our family history.*

—

You are *not* going to be able to change on your own, *so God is going to have to change you,* but He can't change you without you first making the choice. And that's where covenants come in — *covenants are you making the choice and allowing God to change you.*

—

That's what God is going to do for us, *He is not going to let us stay in our comfort zone.* He is going to get us right when we are comfortable, and then He is going to say, *"It is time to take the next step to becoming Godly. Follow me as I lead you through something that is tough, but it is going to get you closer to me."*

—

The whole Exodus story, the story from Egypt to entering the promised land, is what we call an archetypal journey. *It is a journey that is symbolic of the journey that we go on to return to be in God's presence.*

—

It's not intended to be easy. This is going to be a tough trip. A fallen world is a tough trip. Having a fallen nature and dealing with fallen people, that's *a tough trip. But that is by design, because the question becomes, "Are we going to follow God through all of it?"*

—

The Lord is willing to work with us.

—

It sounds like such a harsh thing when God says, "I'm going to strike Miriam with leprosy," *but God immediately heals her.* And then as she goes through the process of being able to be with Israel again, they say, "We won't move on without you. We'll wait, and when you're ready then Israel will move on." *To me that is a story of incredible mercy, not a story of harsh judgment. God does what He needs to do to teach what He needs to teach for the lesson to be learned. And then God says, "Okay I will make it as if it didn't happen, and we'll wait until you're ready and then we'll keep going." That is a very merciful God.*

———

We're all going to cut ourselves off from God again and again and again. I'm not saying don't worry about it, *but don't worry about it too much. It is in the plan, and God has prepared the way for us to overcome that.* Don't beat yourself up and think it is the end of the world.

———

We don't believe Christ when He says, "I can change you." We think our ability to sin can overpower the Atonement. We need to believe Him, that He truly can change us. No matter how silly or wicked or stupid you are, *Christ can change you.* No matter how inconsistent you are, no matter how often you do the same sin over again, no matter how many times you don't do what you know you should do, *Christ can change you and exalt you.* And coming to believe that is one of the greatest things that we need to do in our mortal probation. *The first principle isn't just faith that Christ exists, it is faith that He is our Savior and Redeemer. That He can save us from ourselves and our sins, and redeem us and exalt us.*

———

I don't care what is wrong with you, *it's not more than Christ can fix. It is not beyond His saving and redeeming power. All you have to do is keep coming back to Him.*

———

Don't ever ask yourself *if* you are doing what the children of Israel did; ask yourself *how* you are doing what they did.

——

Sometimes we really beat ourselves up because we are continuing to struggle with a challenge. And my question for you is, *do you really think that you would be done with struggling before you got through mortality? Because I don't think that's the plan. I think the plan is that you have some things that you struggle with all the way through mortality, and Christ will eventually fix it. But it may not be in this life.*

——

As long as you are still trying, then you are making progress.

——

There are going to be times where life bites you, and it is going to take a little while to get to Christ healing you. And you're going to have to walk on some pain and through some pain to get to where Christ is healing you. *But you have to believe that there is something at the end of this that makes it possible for Christ to heal you.*

——

If you look to Christ, you will live. Keep reading your scriptures, keep praying to God through whatever kind of garbage you are going through, *keep doing that. That is one way that you walk to see the brass serpent.*

——

If God is with us, who can stand against us?

——

So what I would hope is that everyone, as they read the Book of Numbers, will think of it as your journey and think of the prophet as your guide. Still, Christ is the one who makes it possible and will deliver you. And see how you can apply that to your life, your journey, the journey of your family, and your covenant community. If we read this with that in mind, the Spirit will whisper to us about things we need to learn from. This will make us more successful in the journey and help us get through the pain of the serpents, help us quit murmuring against God's prophets, and help us get where we're trying to go by believing in Christ. The Lord, through the Holy Ghost, will tell you exactly how that happens in your life if you ask Him while you do this reading.

———

Deuteronomy 6-8;15;18; 29-30;34

Bruce Satterfield

> **Deuteronomy 2:7** *For the Lord thy God hath blessed thee in all the works of thy hand: he knoweth thy walking through this great wilderness: these forty years the Lord thy God hath been with thee; thou hast lacked nothing.*

In Deuteronomy, we have a lot of feeling expressions: love, jealousy, and anger. In our thinking about God, we think we don't like that He gets angry, or the concept of jealous and envious. However, what is the opposite of all of that? *If I didn't have a god that was angry, then what is He?* Apathetic. *These words show us how much God cares. Instead of seeing His feelings as negative, we can see them as confirmation that God is concerned about us.*

——

He *is* a jealous God. He loves us, *of course He wants our love.*

——

God is not in the business of destruction, He is in the business of salvation. So *He always uses His means of destruction to be a means of salvation.*

——

As Christ put God first, and the salvation of His children, so must we. That has to be done on a daily basis and reminding ourselves, what am I doing? Why do I have a job? Why am I going on this vacation? None of which is evil, but in the end it has to somehow be building the Kingdom of Heaven. *It is an inner, mental, hard thing that has to be cognitively done.*

———

When I was young, I read and started to pray more. I had some very powerful spiritual experiences that left me no doubt about the gospel. I was a changed man. The year after I graduated, I went to Israel, and I had a little room in a Palestinian hotel and did my regular schoolwork. Then, at night, I spent hours working on a study on the life of Christ. That year was phenomenal, but I have to say that my testimony was strong. The scholarly side has always been to understand the doctrine, and the doctrine is to understand how to live. I've never let scholarship be the reason, but it's a means to an end.

———

Joshua 1-8; 23-24

George A. Pierce

> ***Joshua 1:9*** *Have not I commanded thee? Be strong and of a good courage; be not afraid, neither be thou dismayed: for the Lord thy God is with thee whithersoever thou goest.*

We are sometimes tasked with very difficult things — at work, our family situations, maybe our callings — but we have this assurance that *God is going to be with us if we are faithful to Him.* We can *"be strong and of a good courage."*

—

What kind of memorials am I setting up for my children? What am I doing in terms of lasting things where they can ask, "Hey dad, what is this about?" and I can tell them about what the Lord did for our family, or for me personally, or for my wife. *How are we memorializing and recounting what the Lord has done for us?*

—

What Joshua needs instead of valor, instead of vivrato, *is obedience.* How many times do we charge into something without even thinking about it? And if we had been obedient to begin with, then things would have fallen into place.

—

If there is a problem with us understanding God's commandments and His actions, then the problem doesn't reside in Him; *the problem is in our limitation of understanding His purposes.* Sometimes we do have to live with that tension and say, *"I don't understand it all now, but in the eternities I'll get it, and that works for me."*

—

What "rest" means here for Joshua, in Genesis, and in our own lives, is not a period of not doing anything; *it is a period of fulfillment.* For us, that means we sometimes have conflicts. And we need that rest, that time, place, and opportunity, *to learn how to be more like the Savior — learn to act as He would act, and take that time and opportunity to fulfill our role of eventually being like Him.*

—

Everything He has promised us, *He is going to come through.*

—

I'll be honest. When I got baptized, I still had only read up through Helaman 12 in the Book of Mormon. I have read the rest of the Book of Mormon between now and then. Being an archaeologist in Israel allowed me the privilege and opportunity to be able to be hands-on in the dirt where some of these things happened and to be able to understand the life of ancient Israel and the Philistines and the Canaanites. And to be able to bring that to my students and say, "These are real people with real problems, and the real solution was obedience to the gospel, or to the law of God," as we see in the Old Testament. Being able to share that with the students is priceless.

———

Judges 2-4; 6-8; 13-16

Dana M. Pike

***Judges 6:14** And the Lord looked upon him and said, Go in this thy might, and thou shalt save Israel from the hand of the Midianites: have not I sent thee?*

Part of the question that the book of Judges raises is *who do we worship and who is our king?* And if we have a human king, what kind of king do we have?

———

He delivers the Israelites again and again. If He did it for them, He can do it for me, too. *He is doing it for me, again and again.*

———

The Lord is going to follow through on what He says if we are willing to participate with Him. There may be challenges, but the Lord will always pull through.

———

If we feel the need for help and reassurance, it's okay to say that; it's okay to be honest and ask for it.

———

Ultimately, *it is the Lord* who is going to fight our battles and who is going to help us be successful in our mortal life.

—

My wife and I have said this to each other: Our covenant relationship with the Lord is the most important thing in our life. Everything grows from that. You're next as my spouse, and everything else proceeds from there: the kids, the grandkids, occupation, ward callings, etc. Listen, I know people who went to graduate school and lost their faith. For me, the academic approach has a lot of value, but it's not an either-or. Take from the best books, study history and geography, learn languages and all these things, and learn even by study and faith. The Doctrine and Covenants is full of divine injunctions to see what's in the world and to have the Holy Spirit as your guide — to choose what's good, helpful, productive, and beneficial, to separate between what's good and what's not, and to choose the good and to reject the rest.

—

Ruth; Samuel 1-3

Gaye Strathearn

> ***Ruth 1:16*** *And Ruth said, Entreat me not to leave thee, or to return from following after thee: for whither thou goest, I will go; and where thou lodgest, I will lodge: thy people shall be my people, and thy God my God.*

Everything that is happening here is to say that *God is aware of you and your needs, and He is responding to you.*

—

This is a great story of men and women working together. It is a great story of women standing shoulder to shoulder to bring about the purposes of God. *This is about real people, like you and I, who are not perfect people. They don't have an idyllic life, but they live their life. And in spite of the difficulties they have, they are trying to do the things of God.*

—

Are there times where I think God has abandoned me? Absolutely. I think we all have experienced that. But this story reminds us again that *God is always in the details. And if we can have faith in Him, not just in the moment but in the long term, we will see the hand of God in our lives if we have eyes to see.* But sometimes it is something we really have to look for.

—

If you have faith, it doesn't mean that you don't have questions. It just means that you are going to keep going with your questions until the time that God can reveal Himself to you in powerful ways.

——

I found that questions were really, really intriguing to me. One of those places, again, where that just changed the way I thought about, read, and studied scriptures. And ever since, I have loved the scriptures. I love the Old Testament. This is one of my favorite books. I'm a person who thinks that context is critically important, not just a nice thing, but it's essential for us to be able to make the connections to how this applies in our lives. Some skills that I learned there have been very important to my study of the scriptures, and I felt the Spirit bless me to see in ways that I haven't seen before. I believe that the Spirit comes to the seekers, not the passive. So, I've got to be looking for questions and reading them so that the Spirit can teach me and direct me.

——

1 Samuel 8-18

Daniel Peterson

1 Samuel 12:14 *If ye will fear the Lord, and serve him, and obey his voice, and not rebel against the commandment of the Lord, then shall both ye and also the king that reigneth over you continue following the Lord your God.*

The gospel, the kingdom, the church, have always got to be out of sync with the world. If they weren't, *that would be a matter of concern.* The point is not to be weird for the sake of being weird, *we should be different. If we are wrapped up with everybody around us, something has gone seriously wrong.*

—

These stories are not just about a time long ago, *they are about us.* If you don't sometimes see yourself in Saul and David, or at least ask yourself whether you can, then you are not reading it correctly.

—

We have to be careful if we are called to a position, that we don't let it go to our heads and we don't think that there is glory in it for us. We have to be careful that we don't become better than others because *we* have been called to that position.

—

I think the Lord gives us commandments to teach us obedience. Is it so much about the cup of coffee? Probably not. But it's the attitude that *you* can be exempt from the Lord's rules. When we start to shave the rules little by little, soon there are no rules. That's what the Lord is doing with the Israelites and that's what the Lord is doing with us — He is trying to teach His people the principle of exactness and obedience.

———

I would hear Hugh Nibbley say, even privately, "We know so little about what the Lord is talking about, what the Lord is doing, and how the Lord thinks. *We just don't know much of anything. There is no reason for any of us to be vein, because we are so pathetically small compared to the universe.*"

———

If we go into something thinking we already know everything, *we close ourselves off to learning anything*

———

If you put your trust in the arm of the flesh, eventually somebody will come along with more flesh. For that reason, we must put our trust in God.

—

Bring your strengths to the kingdom. We're good at some things, we're not as good at others. *We don't have to be the other guy.* We can bring what we have. That's what David did, he didn't allow himself to be made into something he wasn't. If you try to do something very different, then you may lose all together.

—

These are such powerful human stories. Tragic stories. Some doctrine in it, but mostly *it's about behavior. It's about how we obey the Lord, how we deal with the blessings the Lord has given us, and who takes the credit for the blessings that we get in our achievements. That is relevant to every one of us.*

—

I think the scriptures are so rich and they're so profound. And that's one of the reasons that I have a testimony of them, is that you can go back to them time and time again at different points in your life or different situations in your life, and they'll mean something very different to you. I have an old set of scriptures that I had when I was a teenager. And I see the passages that I marked in those scriptures then, and they're good passages. But I see that I passed over passages that now mean everything to me. And so, that's part of my testimony — the scriptures are true and the time spent in studying them and not just reading them, but pondering them and seeking to liken them unto ourselves, is time well spent. There's a treasure trove of wisdom as well as divine guidance and doctrine and everything else in them. I bear that testimony, in the name of Jesus Christ. Amen.

——

2 Samuel 5-12, 1 Kings 3-11

Michael Goodman

> ***1 Kings 6:12–13*** *Concerning this house which thou art in building, if thou wilt walk in my statutes, and execute my judgments, and keep all my command-ments to walk in them; then will I per-form my word with thee, which I spake unto David thy father: and I will dwell among the children of Israel, and will not forsake my people Israel.*

For us to get what we need out of the story, we need to make sure we are seeing it as the Lord has actually revealed it. What did it mean to David? What did it mean to Bathsheba? In their context, not our context. And *then* we have to ask, *"What does the Lord want me to take from this?"*

—

Hopefully we can give grace and, with David and everyone in our lives, *acknowledge mistakes without negating all the good.* Don't define people by their worst moments or *by what others say* are their worst moments.

—

You have to know the *character* of God to be able to correctly interpret any scriptural story, modern or ancient. *We know God is loving, forgiving, and merciful.* So, we know Uzah is not damned.

—

It's all about that relationship. When we keep that relationship-bound covenant connected to Christ, *it not only protects us from the errors we might make, it gives us the power to do all the good that the Lord needs and wants us to do, and that we need to do.* So, it comes back to, *are we keeping that covenant connection, that binding tie, with God?*

———

Don't try to go outside the sphere that the lord has given you to work. If you're the Sunday school teacher, stop trying to be the bishop. Stay in your stewardship.

———

We do not believe in prophetic infallibility, *but we do believe in God's infallibility* and we believe that God directs His prophets. Not that they can never say or think in error, *but if they are in error, it won't be our job to correct them — it will be the Lord's job to correct them.*

———

Most of the time, even when we are struggling, we are not trying to hurt another person. Our intent isn't evil, *but our actions can be hurtful.* In this case, if David and his wife would have *sought to understand what the other person was feeling and thinking and why, and empathized with them, even if there were some parts of it that weren't based on what they intended. Just by feeling understood, it lowers the temperature* and then allows couples to begin to talk through issues in a way that leads to what most of us experience, but instead without all the pain — a reconciliation.

—

This principle is so powerful: *When we are sensitive to the promptings of the Spirit, God will not let us proceed too far without a warning impression.* I testify that God is leading His prophets. No, they are not perfect, and yes, they can have their own opinions. *But the Lord is not going to allow His servants the prophets to guide us and take us off the path in a way that is going to endanger our progression toward God. Trust the Lord to guide.*

—

When we make mistakes, generally, God doesn't have to lightning bolt us; He lets the consequences of our actions teach us the errors of our ways.

———

Again, what we see with David and Solomon is they start to recognize their need for and dependence on God. He is realizing the difference between him and God. *"Who am I, God, in comparison with you?" Isn't that the humility that we hope all of us will exemplify?*

———

Sometimes it is not going to work the way we think or want. *But if we truly come to know God* and *we know His character* and *His relationship to us* and *His perfections, we can trust that He knows best* how to move his own work forward and how to move us forward toward our own exaltation.

———

The question isn't if you saw something, and therefore, you are guilty; it is *did you see something, and what did you do next?* What David did next becomes the problem.

———

The only way Satan can get a good latter-day saint to make this kind of a serious error is to separate that latter-day saint from the Spirit of God. As David's relationship with God became more tenuous, his wisdom, his decision making, his choices, they began to follow more of the natural man than the Spirit of God. That tragedy of allowing ourselves to disconnect from God is the way that Satan has the greatest chance of getting in and encouraging us to go down this horrifically tragic rabbit hole.

———

None of us are immune to the mistakes we can make. That is why it is so crucial to stay connected to God and to recognize when we begin to disconnect.

———

Yes, the Lord has asked us, male and female, for modesty; but someone else's immodesty is never reason for our violation of a principle or commandment. *We have to take responsibility.*

—

The problem is not sexuality, it is not the physical body; the body is meant to be exalted.

—

It is very clear, looking at it even from a secular view — immortality does not correlate with good outcomes.

—

This plea for an understanding heart pleases God. *The Lord is saying to us, "I want to be your God, I want you to be my child.* Not just in a literal sense, but *I want to walk together."* So when we plead to Him, *"God, I want to listen. I want to learn,"* He is so pleased.

—

God is always more gracious to us than we could ever hope or deserve. But there is always a caveat. *There is always a covenantal "if then."* That is how the blessings of God always come to us — *based on our honoring our agency and using our agency in a way that ties us and binds us to God.*

———

The prophet has been pleading with us to have regular experiences with God. He doesn't want us to just be a churchy people or a religious people. We aren't seeking to be bound to the church, *we are seeking to be bound to God through that covenantal relationship. That happens as we daily seek to see the fingerprints of God in our life.*

———

Satan is pretty good at his deceptions and at his imitations. If we want to stay safe from the imitations the world or Satan would give, *we have to have experiences with God.*

———

David and Solomon both erred on these very matters of the family and marriage. That is why it is so tragic, *because those are the two areas that will have the strongest impact on their eternal destiny.* To understand our theology, we cannot become as our Eternal Parents without an eternal companion by our side. And hence the commandment, not just the suggestion, that we marry in the Lord's house to someone of the opposite gender whom we can spend eternity with. It is the Lord's commandment that we approach sexual relations and approach marriage as the Lord has commanded. *Not because God doesn't love others, not because being single is wrong, but because this is the purpose and the process of life.*

———

It's not the temporal consequences that matter the most, it is the eternal consequences that matter most.

———

We are anxiously seeking to help our students understand that our nature is God's nature, and God's nature is relational. We are intended to be in relation to God, and our eternal destiny is based on living true to our eternal marriage covenants.

—

The Lord doesn't say, "I required perfection yesterday," the Lord *"requires the heart and the willing mind."*

—

God has promised that nobody will be denied every blessing that He has promised His children based on anything outside of their control. *You and I can know that if we stay covenant-connected to God, we will lose nothing. We will become as our Father and Mother in Heaven. We will receive every blessing God has promised all of His children.*

—

I love Doctrine and Covenants 64:34: "The Lord requires the heart and the willing mind." He didn't say, "I required perfection yesterday." What He needs us to do is to catch the eternal vision of what sexuality, gender, marriage, and family are according to God and then do our very best to pattern our lives after that. Realizing that none of us will do it perfectly, and also learning that, in this life, not all will experience these things in their fullness. And that God has promised — and this I think is so crucial. God has promised that nobody will be denied every blessing that He has promised His children based on anything that is outside of their control. You and I can know that if we stay covenant-connected to God, we will lose nothing. We will become as our Father and Mother in Heaven. We will receive every blessing God has promised all his children.

———

1 Kings 17-19

Camille F. Olson

1 Kings 19:11–12 And he said, Go forth, and stand upon the mount before the Lord. And, behold, the Lord passed by, and a great and strong wind rent the mountains, and brake in pieces the rocks before the Lord; but the Lord was not in the wind: and after the wind an earthquake; but the Lord was not in the earthquake: And after the earthquake a fire: but the Lord was not in the fire: and after the fire a still small voice.

Isn't Elijah being taught this same principle, *that His survival depends on him relying on the Lord?* Don't *we* have that with Fast Sunday? The reminder that *it is not bread alone that we need to sustain us, but that our souls need nourishment.*

—

We think we have a testimony, but sometimes it takes even greater challenges. And the way the Lord can rescue us in those challenges is to say, *"Okay I think I got it now."*

—

The way the Lord often answers our prayers *is by someone that we might not ever expect.*

—

He is with us in our extremities. If we let Him, He will take us to where no one else can help us and then we turn completely to Him.

—

Anytime that we have felt alone, as a lone believer in an environment where people are saying, "You have no idea what you are talking about," this is not true. *There is Elijah.*

——

The journey is sometimes too great for us. He stretches us. We see miracles, and His grace makes us equal to what is needed, but there is sometimes an added pouring out of love and grace and mercy upon us that remind us that He is so aware and He recognizes our hurt and our discouragement. I think it is in those times, when it is more quiet, and we feel like, "Is he there?" that we get these little gentle feelings of His awareness that help us come through.

——

Elijah and the widow of Zarephath remind me that even without having all the answers, we can know, *because of what He has done for us in the past, He will continue to help us in the future. We can have that rock-solid commitment to follow Him.*

—

There is a time that Elijah will experience where it seems like God is silent. *The Lord sometimes answers us with silence, and we need to be prepared for that as well.*

—

I think one of the most powerful messages that comes through here is Jehovah's awareness of all of his children, whether they be of the House of Israel or outside the House of Israel. There is good that comes from the widow of Zarephath that will inspire a prophet. So, whatever station we are in, whatever our circumstances, when we have an opportunity to help when someone asks for help, we would be willing to step forward, whether it is feeding a hundred prophets in caves or giving the very last out of our cupboard. But it is in those extremities that we discover him and that we are not afraid of what he desires to show us, with a still, small voice.

———

2 Kings 2-7

Krystal Pierce

> ***2 Kings 2:14*** *And he took the mantle of Elijah that fell from him, and smote the waters, and said, Where is the Lord God of Elijah? And when he also had smitten the waters, they parted hither and thither: and Elisha went over.*

We may not know where everybody has been scattered, but the Lord knows *exactly* where every single person is. That is why *He* is the gatherer.

—

If a prophet or apostle or somebody says something and you immediately want to balk and say, "Woah I don't know about that." Then that's a perfect time to stop and think, "Why am I getting defensive or balking at this?" It's a good indicator to really think about it.

—

We never should put limits on the Lord, ever. And sometimes when we say, "Oh, this miracle can't happen to me," or "It's too hard," if we actually step back and think, "What am I saying? Things are too hard for God? For the Lord?" *They never are. And so it's us. It's our faith and our understanding that needs to be worked on.*

—

Who are *you* turning to when *you* are in trouble? Don't forget, *God has the power.* He is the one who can help you. *He is the one who knows your story and who you are and everything that you are,* not your phone or the internet or celebrities.

——

If you have broken a covenant, *you can return. You can heal that break.*

——

When we find things like this, outside extra biblical information or archaeology, *it is not meant to make us more faithful. Because faith doesn't come from provable facts, faith comes from belief. It comes from believing even though we don't have the facts.*

——

The Lord cares about everyone — whole cities, one woman, everybody. The oil, the Atonement of Jesus Christ, *it covers everybody.*

——

Sometimes it is not up to the opinions of others. In fact, very rarely is it up to the opinions of others. And when people question us, or we begin to question ourselves, we can be like Elijah and say, *"I know who I am, and I know who I represent."*

—

When this debt slavery issue comes up, we are meant to think of the Lord as our Kinsman Redeemer. He is the one who comes in. He redeems us from our sin, from our debt. He is the one who paid it off. He saves us.

—

It doesn't matter your age, your gender, your status, or your wealth; *you always can have these opportunities come up where you can share your beliefs, talk about the prophet, or say, "You can be healed from whatever problem you have, whether it is physical or spiritual."*

—

Sometimes we are so ready to accept others' miracles — big miracles of healing or getting exactly what they need — and then when it comes to us, we say, "That would never happen to me," or "I don't have big miracles in my life," when in reality it is a matter of believing in our own miracles and recognizing the miracles in our own lives.

——

Sometimes we want things to be complicated and difficult and hard, but so many times it's not like that. *The Lord asks simple things of us that we can do, and we will be healed.*

——

He is a fighter. *He wants us to win.* All we have to do is ask Him for help — help in opening our eyes to realize our full true potential, help realizing that we are not alone and that there are way more people who are helping us than there are against us. *He is on our side.* This is part of the gathering, making sure everybody understands their true identity as children of God.

——

The hosts of heaven are meant to remind us that His armies and His support and *His angels are way more than any army or enemy that is coming at us.* Sometimes we may feel we are surrounded and there is nothing we can do, and so we need to pray to recognize all the help and support and love that the Lord gives to us. Now, as our protector, *He is going to fight for us. These chariots and horses are meant to show us that He will fight for us and that He is there for us.*

———

Miracles are for entire cities *but also for individuals. They can come in any size, shape, or form, which makes it about us learning to recognize them.* God cares about every single one of His children, and a big part of it is opening our eyes, seeing the miracles in our own lives, realizing our true potential, and that God loves every single one of us.

———

We need to pray and ask for our eyes to be open in the same way that this servant's eyes are opened, in the same way that the woman with the child had her eyes opened. And she was a believer. Sometimes we need that extra push, that little extra help. Or like Naaman, washing in the river — just a little reminder, every once in a while, that we're not alone. I think the Lord is there, His armies are on both sides of the veil, and our eyes need to be opened to these miracles.

———

2 Kings 17-25

Joshua Sears

> ***2 Kings 18: 19*** *And Rab-shakeh said unto them, Speak ye now to Hezekiah, Thus saith the great king, the king of Assyria, What confidence is this wherein thou trustest?*

You have to scatter in order to gather. The Lord is playing the long game.

———

"What confidence is this wherein thou trusteth?" That is a great question for us today. *What do you trust in?* This is a powerful story about how you can have these voices in the world that are actively working to undermine trust, whether that's in the prophet, in church leaders, or in God. These people are doing it strategically, where they know it is going to hurt the most. And that's when we get to choose: *who* are we going to listen to? *What* are we going to trust in?

———

All of us, we might not have Assyrians on our doorstep, but all of us have those prayers: *"Save us,* we are desperate. We have tried to do our best. There is nothing else we can do, no one else can save us. *Please,* save us."

———

These moments do come where you have to ask yourself, it's not theoretical anymore, it's not abstract theology, it's push comes to shove here: *Do I believe the gospel?* Am I willing to put my money where my mouth is or put my family's life on the line? *That* is what Hezekiah was dealing with here.

——

Hezekiah is a reminder that if you've got a human leader, as good as they might be, they are going to eventually disappoint you. If you look hard enough or wait long enough, whether it is Joseph Smith or your bishop or somebody, they will disappoint you. *They're not perfect.* But the Savior, of course, is going to do everything that they can do but perfectly, and we can trust Him not to stumble and let us down.

——

We might not be living life perfectly. But as we listen and read the scriptures, we can recognize the difference between what the scriptures are teaching and something in our own life. And we can humble ourselves enough to conform to what the scriptures teach, that the Lord recognizes that and says, "You know what, it doesn't matter what you did in the past, I am pleased that you are making the change now that you know better."

—

Access to scriptures is not our problem today. They are on our phones and on our shelves, but opening them up and actually reading them and feasting on the word of Christ... that's the real challenge. And when we do, it can be like a rediscovery as *we find there is a feast waiting for us* that maybe we haven't had in a while.

—

God has a long game. He is not making promises to these people and then everything is going to be ruined. In fact, even though they are wicked and have some major setbacks and all sorts of destruction and calamity, they can't ultimately thwart God's plans. He is always going to find a way to use Israel to accomplish His purposes, no matter how bad they blow it along the way. So, the theological takeaway here is that *God is still in charge. He is moving the chess board in ways that we can't comprehend and with the sight that goes beyond what we can see, and He is going to make everything turn out the way it is supposed to be.*

———

All your losses will be made up to you in the resurrection, provided you continue faithful. By the vision of the Almighty, I have seen it. And I hear the power there, in Joseph's words. That man knew loss, and he knew suffering, but he saw and knew perfectly that every promised blessing could be ours, whether in this life or the next. So, if you're going through one of those times right now, please do not give up. Trust that Heavenly Father will help you. We have the testimony of the prophets and the witness of people in the Bible there who went before us that God will not abandon us or forsake us. We'll have these Hezekiah last-minute miracles come into our lives, and it might come later, it might come sooner. But Heavenly Father is someone we can trust. He will never break trust with us.

———

Ezra 1; 3-7, Nehemiah 2; 4-6; 8

Jared W. Ludlow

> ***Ezra 5:11*** *And thus they returned us answer, saying, We are the servants of the God of heaven and earth, and build the house that was builded these many years ago, which a great king of Israel builded and set up.*

People can go through the same experiences and have different reactions, based on how they enter into that.

—

We shouldn't be scared of looking at other resources when we have questions. But of course, the scriptures first and foremost can give us answers, and more importantly, they will open the door for direct experiences with God Himself.

—

Our personal worship is very important and vital, but there is also a community aspect to our worship. We are part of a broader community, both a Latter-Day Saint community, a Christian community, and even a believer-in-God community. It's those interactions in the broader community that can help strengthen us, where we can serve and love others.

—

It is with the Lord's help we can do what we need to do.

—

We can learn that it's important to stick to what
we know is right and hold firm to that foundation of Christ, even with the temptations
or the efforts of others to call us away. With
our testimonies, we can know, "I am in a solid
place. I don't want to get on a shaky foundation
or sandy foundation, I want to hold onto that
firm foundation."

—

When I think of my children and their spouses,
I hope they always focus on having the temple
at the center of their worship. And again, it
starts with personal worship — if we're married with our spouses, then with our families.
But then we're serving in the temple a much
broader community, whether that's extended
family, ancestors beyond the veil, or names that
we don't know but can do service for. And that's
where I draw strength from, participating in
this wider work centered in the temple.

—

Esther

Ariel Silver

> **Esther 4:14** *For if thou altogether holdest thy peace at this time, then shall there enlargement and deliverance arise to the Jews from another place; but thou and thy father's house shall be destroyed: and who knoweth whether thou art come to the kingdom for such a time as this?*

The Book of Esther is not just a story written in exile about the experience of the Jews in exile; *it is really THE story of exile in an existential sense, in the sense of our mortal lives being an experience of exile.* It's a place where we are separated from our spiritual home and we are left to find our way. And in the process of that exile, we have been pulled apart from the things that most deeply identify us as divine beings. *We are now living in an experience of duality, of opposition in all things. The only way for that exile to end is for a return to the presence of God and a reconciliation with God, a unity.* This experience, that in the mortal realm feels dualistic, complex, and multifaceted, that eventually should result in a reunification, *does. This book is so important because it lays out that entire movement, from separation and life in exile to a story of redemption.*

—

The book of Esther is not always included in sacred canons like Jewish, Catholic, Orthodox, or Protestant, because they couldn't figure out if it is a book of scripture because God's name isn't mentioned. *But that's because God is hidden in the same way that God is veiled from us in our mortal experience.*

———

The name of Esther in Hebrew means "I hide myself." *Embedded in the very name of the book is the place where God resides in the text.* In Deuteronomy, it says, "I shall hide my face." We are taught that there are times where God will hide himself from us.

———

There are other records of the exilic experience. Jeremiah writes about it, Isaiah writes about it, others write about it as well, but they mostly perceive exile as something to be endured, something to be survived, something for which we hope for a resolution. They don't really want it to endure longer than it has to. In the Book of Esther *she sees it as an opportunity,* even in the face of a really severe, life-threatening situation where a decree against their lives has been placed. *But she sees exile as an opportunity to develop capacities to grow.*

———

Across the span of these chapters, the female character of Esther changes. She evolves, and she progresses. It's a heroine's story. She comes into her own. As her purpose comes more clear, her power, her knowledge, and her understanding also grows. Her capacity to act and do things that are going to work toward her salvation personally and the salvation of other people increases.

———

There is a play between whether God is present, whether He is absent, or whether He is asking us to act of our own accord — to be anxiously engaged in good causes and not waiting for God's prompt for every worthy thing we are to do, or whether we are, at times, in a position of advent to wait for His direction.

———

In Esther, almost entirely unique in the whole canon of scripture, we see a woman who changes, who progresses spiritually, and who takes upon herself a pretty serious mantle and is willing to risk her life.

———

It's a book of tremendous hope. Against impossible odds, these Jews succeed. And they overcome the oppression that they faced and they become victorious. It's a story of tremendous hope and joy.

———

We are all in spiritual exile from our Heavenly home and we are all searching to achieve that reunification. We, like the Jews in this story and to this day, live in the face of challenges, of threats, and of difficulties. *We all need to know that God can deliver us and that we can be redeemed. We can overcome the difficulties that we face.*

———

It's a tremendous book about inspiration and revelation; a book about courage in face of impossible odds, about reliance on God for detailed guidance to make it through the quagmires of our lives. A book about spiritual creativity in developing very carefully inspired solutions. A book about transforming complex situations into opportunities to exercise greater faith and greater resolve. A book about ways to engage with threats and injustices that we face. And ways to turn from anger and bitterness and revenge to mercy.

———

We don't go after retribution. It's not an eye for an eye or a tooth or a tooth. There is a higher law that is already at work in this text, and we see it in the kind of restraint that is exercised both as Esther approaches this problem and finds solutions. And even when they are on the cusp of victory, she makes it clear to "not lay waste and not take their spoils."

———

We have moments where we can have influence that is righteous. *We can shift the narrative in such a way that it brings blessings to ourselves, to those in our care, and to those we have stewardship.*

———

If you don't follow the promptings of the Holy Ghost, He will inspire somebody else. The work He needs accomplished will be accomplished by someone else. God would like to give that opportunity to you, but it's your choice to respond to it or not respond to it. But whatever decision you make, the word of God will not be forted. *The Lord will save us. We will be redeemed.*

———

Against all the oppression we face, Esther is a moment where we are reminded that in the end, *God will prevail. All will be well.*

———

We have to choose to see the miracles in our lives. We have to choose to see that experience as something that involved the hand of the Lord, not something that just randomly occurred but something that involved His mercy for us — His great and profound love for us.

———

Whatever destruction you might visit on someone else, ultimately you destroy yourself; that's
the real punishment. It is self-destructive to seek
one's own self elevation.

—

The experience for everyone will be different.
But we will have those situations where it will
require a reexamination of what it is that we
know spiritually. How am I going to respond?
Where am I going to put my confidence and
my faith and my energy? What am I made of
spiritually? What am I willing to do in order to
receive the guidance that I need to navigate my
way through a situation that feels impossible?

—

In the Book of Esther, we have the experience of a woman who does something at *a redemptive level* on behalf of others. That is not tied to motherhood and is not tied to the bearing of children. Just about every other example in scripture is an elevation of the female as a mother, as a teacher, as a nurturer, someone who provides continuity, strength, wisdom, and insight from generation to generation. Those things are all tremendously important, *but it is also important to recognize that that is not the only role that women fill in life. They have great gifts to give in other realms as well.* Esther provides us a very powerful example of a woman apart from motherhood who does tremendous work and carefully seeks out guided, inspired solutions that are going to bless and benefit her people.

———

I remember, of course, the beautiful passage in Romans. Nothing, nothing, absolutely nothing, can separate us from the love of God — nothing, nothing. This love is constant and unconditional. However much we feel in exile at any point in our lives, we are never separated from the love of God. I demonstrated a life lived in belief, even if I didn't have all the answers. And there are many things that I have on the back burners, wanting responses for many things. Even if I didn't have the answer to every question, a life lived in hope, a life lived in belief, a life lived in the scriptures was a life that would be a constant spark and a constant inspiration for me. And it would feed me intellectually and spiritually. The things that I was doing spiritually would also feed me intellectually and emotionally.

———

Job

Adam Miller

> **Job 1:21** *And said, Naked came I out of my mother's womb, and naked shall I return thither: the Lord gave, and the Lord hath taken away; blessed be the name of the Lord.*

With Job we get to witness, in a really raw and unfiltered way that is unusual for scripture, what it looks like to wrestle with God, not knowing what God is doing or why, and to see that as part of your religion rather than a departure from your religion.

—

What are the grounds for your faithfulness? Are you faithful to God because you hope to get something out of it? Is it kind of quid pro quo, or is your faithfulness to God ground in the kind of love that is not conditioned on God giving you what you thought you wanted?

—

I think we can look at Job as a case study: what it looks like to mourn with those who mourn or fail to mourn with those who mourn, depending on how we evaluate Job's friends and how they mourn with him.

—

The silence is beautiful and, in lots of ways, necessary. But also, despite the difficulty and the trouble of the talking and the wrestling, it can get us to where we need to be.

—

The lesson that I take from the book of Job is that *we are always wrong when we think that suffering equates straightforwardly to punishment.*

—

The very practice of religion is not so much about finding a way to get God to give you what you want. *But instead, the very essence of religion is to mourn, to find a way to handle loss* — and to handle that loss together in a way that can redeem it, even if we can't roll it back.

—

It's tempting to think that religion is about always making sure we know what everything means, always being able to assign meaning to everything that happens. But the older I have gotten, *the more it seems to me that I would prefer to describe religion as the ongoing business of grappling with things that simply lack meaning.*

———

I think the book of Job wants us to feel, along with Job, what he is feeling and wants us to put ourselves in his shoes, to wrestle with the thing he is wrestling with.

———

Usually in the scriptures, what we primarily mean by the word "faith" is *trust.* We don't mean by faith a willingness to believe things that we don't know for sure, *what we mean is something much more like my willingness to place my trust in another person.*

———

Faith is that tension between declarations of despair while maintaining a willingness to follow; the willingness to stick with it in a relationship with another person, even though things haven't gone the way that you wanted.

———

Despair is the raw material for prayer. It's the stuff of which our relationship with God is made, *not the stuff that you have to get rid of before you can have a relationship with God.*

———

The thing that God is promising is a kind of peace *that operates at a different level* than the coming and going of our fortunes in this world.

———

Another one of the big takeaways of the book of Job has to do with how we think about the relationship between morals and commandments and suffering. It's tempting to think about it in the way that the natural man does — as a punishment for failing to keep the commandments. But I think we are better off thinking about it from the other direction, *in terms of thinking about the commandments as God's remedy for suffering.* Morality, commandments, God's law, those are responses to suffering, not explanations for suffering. Job drives home this point: *You can't use morality to explain suffering, but you should and must use morality to respond to suffering.*

—

It's easy to get the impression as you go through God's discourse with Job that God is, in some sense, chastening Job and telling him, "You shouldn't be asking all these questions," and He kind of does that. But when He's done, God says Job was right for asking those questions, and his friends are wrong for telling him not to ask, and he better repent.

—

Job's friends were wrong to think that suffering is the kind of thing that can be deserved.

—

I feel like I have become increasingly sensitive to the ways that books can open doors unto God, but I've also become increasingly sensitive to how books can be a way of avoiding God. Both of those are constant temptations. I'm interested in the Book of Job, especially because I'm interested in God. I'm not especially interested in religion. What I'm interested in at the end of the day is God. This is what I'm looking for. There are a lot of things I don't know or understand about my own religion or my own experience of religion. My sense of my own ignorance has only grown in that respect. I came to religion looking for God, and I am a Latter-day Saint and will till the day I die be a Latter-day Saint, because this is where God has shown himself to me.

—

Psalms 1-46

Shon Hopkin

Psalms 31:1 *In thee, O Lord, do I put my trust; let me never be ashamed: deliver me in thy righteousness.*

David understood the power of music; it's not just about the power of the word.

—

Hymn singing is a time when you're saying words and feeling things in your own little space, and where the person all the way across the room is singing with their heart, and then you have heavenly choirs, *and you are all giving exactly the same message.* It's heaven and each of us as a congregation *pleading* with the Lord. We are each worshiping individually, but all of us with one heart and one mind.

—

You'll find places in the psalms that just speak to you in those times when you desperately need peace.

—

If you don't have places to go when you are devastated, and when you are unable to connect to the more cerebral portions of thinking about the gospel, *find a favorite psalm.* Let David's own angst, *let the psalmist's own sense of the challenges of mortality, speak for you.*

——

Jesus loves the psalms.

——

We know God loves music because of the way it resonates with us. We as His children are built that way, and I don't know that we fully know why, but we are built to love and be changed and comforted and strengthened by these kinds of things.

——

I think the psalms are trying to accomplish putting it all aside and joining the community of God together. And we are of one heart and one mind, and *that* can change us.

—

That's *the* cry: "It's not that I don't believe, I am trying to believe. But *how long* is this going to last? Can I handle this?" To hear that prayer repeated in the psalms over and over again is really powerful.

—

Well, I don't know if I've done that very well, but the psalm just sings. And it sings Jesus Christ and the great redeeming work that He performed that happened in a specific time and place, but it had an impact across time and space and has blessed all.

—

Life is wonderful and rich, and it's good and…
wow, mortality can be a bear sometimes. And
navigating those feelings and having a place
I can go that is going to help express that, for
me, is really cathartic and really healing. That's
what I think God wants from our religious worship. *"Let me heal you. I want you to be healthy. I want
you to be mine. I want you to be okay. Even though life
is difficult, and that's okay too, come through that and
reunite with me on the other side. Let me offer you my
hand — my hand of love."*

———

Isn't that beautiful? As the Savior is giving us
that sense that, "I see you. I know you. I will
meet you where you are," *He is also saying, "And
in the midst of your suffering, I will triumph and you
will triumph."*

———

The way I like to think of it is like when you have a child that just has to go through something difficult, and they have to do it. *You can't take that away from them. They have to walk through that difficult thing, and they have to know that they've had the strength to do it.* Maybe it's rare, these moments where you let them experience, but you are there. *You are watching, you are loving, and you are cheering them on. You are aching with them. And so, Elder Holland's affirmation: God doesn't leave us alone, but it does feel like we're alone at times. That is part of this divine process as well.*

—

This is what I love about being a Christian believing in Christ, is that He comforts me. He meets me, He understands sorrow, and He gives me hope that I will triumph after all things.

—

We need a god who meets us where we are, and may I just testify, give my sense of this. As you're reading this with Come Follow Me, seek diligently. These scriptures might save your life someday, knowing them and loving them. *There may come a time where you are just ashes, so to speak, emotionally. And you just aren't strong enough to know where to go to get comfort and to get help. And the psalms may be that which gets you through the dark hours of the night,* which were given by an ancient Israelite, who I love, for the depth of soul that is expressed here and for this witness of God and God's mercy. *And I hope you find something that will be that tether for you. And if the time comes when you desperately need a tether, you may find it right here in these weeks' readings.*

—

Early on, to see the incredible interconnectedness of the teachings of the prophets over time is so deeply satisfying — as I've said, probably too many times now, across time and space. How beautiful is it to see those messages interweave and support each other and for a Latter-day Saint reader to recognize God is God? And the God of the Hebrew Bible is the God of the Restoration, and they are one. And it all folds together into this grand witness of what God has been trying to accomplish from the beginning to the end. And even though there are differences in the ancient world, to see the grand unity of the message is something that resonates in my soul as someone who believes deeply in the ministry and the mission of the Savior, Jesus Christ.

—

Psalms 49-86

Eric Huntsman

*> **Psalms 62:5–6** My soul, wait thou only upon God; for my expectation is from him. He only is my rock and my salvation: he is my defence; I shall not be moved.*

The Psalms represent the *very human response to the word of God.*

—

Our prayers are just words if they're not truly directed to God. Our hymns are just music if they're not singing praise to God.

—

If prayer is the soul's most sincere desire, then music is perhaps *its most earnest expression;* it's the way we can really carry our feeling into the words.

—

Poetry is concentrated, creative, and evocative use of language. *Poetry can say more in four or five words than professionals can in a paragraph. It's concentrated,* it's creative, it's expressing things not in your day to day speech.

—

One of the reasons people like poetry is because it's able to bring to the surface or distill out of us or summon out of us feelings, whether they be emotional feelings, as a lot of love poetry does, or spiritual feelings. And that's what I love about the Psalms — *they're able to pull out of me the feelings of my heart.*

—

But really, the block of reading for this week *is really about us* — about our experiences, our joy, our sorrow, our discouragement, our heartaches, and our need for God.

—

We have to let ourselves be *completely crushed.* We have to go through the cycle, and then He will create something new.

—

If you're praying for help for the day in the morning, and you're reviewing your day with the Lord and thanking Him for the blessings of the evening, *why not in the middle of it?* When you're in the middle of the challenges that need the help, and you're in the middle of the joys, and you've got the gratitude. This Psalm says that we can turn from feeling abandoned and overwhelmed by our enemies. We can call upon God, and He'll save us. Why? *Because we're going to call upon Him evening, morning, and noon — all times of the day. He hath delivered my soul in peace from the battle that was against me.*

———

When it says that God is "terrible," it's the idea that He's filling you with the fear of the Lord in the sense of you're awestruck by Him. When you say our God is an awesome god, it's a god that fills us with awe. Now, if you're not right with God, it will feel like terror; it will be fear. But if you're right with him, it'll be, *"wow."*

———

If I'm not feeling close to the Lord, if I'm not feeling worshipful, if I'm not feeling it, I read something like this aloud and it gets me in that mode. And then I can kneel down and offer my own prayer.

———

Worship is an experience with God that transforms the worshiper. If you're not in the presence of God, you don't *feel* His presence. If you don't feel that you're in the presence of God, or singing to God or performing a ritual, an ordinance in front of God, *it's not transforming you. I don't think God wants us to worship Him and praise Him because He needs his ego stroked; it's because He knows it changes us.* It makes us turn away from our own ego and our own strength, so called, even our own weaknesses, our own failings, and look to something higher and better that we aspire to.

———

I think some of these psalms, including the cursing psalms and the complaint psalms, provide a template. *If you can't be honest with God, who knows everything about you, who can you be honest with? Of all the people to put on a show for, God is not it. And yet, we do.* And I think what the psalms are showing us is to be honest with God, say, "God, I'm upset. God, I'm hurt. God, I want him to fail. God, I want her to love me," and get out of your system and work through it. And the Spirit will lead you along, and then you'll suddenly change.

—

The Lord, when we repent, He forgives us and He forgets. *And we don't forget. We need to forgive ourselves, but we don't always forget.* That's because we need to learn from the mistakes we've made and have that memory, not always a happy one, serve as an encouragement not to turn back to that kind of behavior.

—

If He's our Father, we should really talk to him; and I think the psalms are giving us the template for that. *We can talk to Him about the good, bad, and the ugly.*

—

Worship is not just an earth thing, it's not just a one-time thing; it's a forever and eternity and everywhere thing.

—

The prototypes, if you will, or object lessons of rebelliousness, *can be ourselves in our own lives.* Look back at periods in our lives when we weren't as faithful. How will that encourage us to be better now?

—

Some people say, "Are you a theologian?" I say, "No, *I'm an exegete. I study text.*" *I'm a practitioner.* I'm not the one who sits around and theologizes, if that's a verb; *I practice the gospel.*

—

It's okay to just read the scriptures and feel the Spirit, even if you don't have a particular message from them. I think sometimes we almost set ourselves up for frustration. We become almost too utilitarian. "What is it going to do for me? How is this going to better me?" *Well, maybe it's just going to transform you because it's going to help you feel God.*

—

We're not all the same, we're not all singing the same part, but we're still one.

—

I think we have these little experiences in life which teach us about our souls. *And what we don't know on a conscious level, our spirits are feeling,* like missing our Heavenly Parents, missing those who've gone before, and those who haven't come yet.

—

So, my son has autism because of a genetic throw of the dice, but he's probably not going to marry and have children. I remember shortly after his diagnosis of autism I was crying and said, "Heavenly Father…" I said, "All these righteous desires I had for my son to serve a mission and marry in the temple, be a father… They're not going to happen. Why is this happening to my son?" And kicker, I said, "He's my only son." Now, this was the Thursday before Easter. And an audible voice came to me and said, "What about my Only Son?" We spend so much time saying we want to be more like Jesus, but when the hardships and the sorrows come, we're like, "No, not me, Lord, take it back." So Sam taught me a lot about accepting the will of the Lord, and it also broke my heart open for people whose lives would not be typical, but I knew how much God loved him.

—

Psalms 102-150

Michael McLean

Psalm 105:1 *O give thanks unto the Lord; call upon his name: make known his deeds among the people. Sing unto him, sing Psalms unto him: talk ye of all his wondrous works. Glory ye in his holy name: let the heart of them rejoice that seek the Lord. Seek the Lord, and his strength: seek his face evermore.*

So many times I think with songs that if we're sitting there and the tune doesn't resonate, we miss the power of the lyric. We miss the power of the message.

—

When I take the spirit of a song and try to turn it into a song of my own and interpret it, I don't feel too bad about not singing the words exactly as written in the King James version. I'm trying to get to the heart of it so that I can keep repeating that message to myself.

—

I don't think that God is insecure and needs us to praise Him so He'll feel okay. *He's never been unsteady. I don't think He's ever been unsure.* He's not waiting for my praise to make His day. But if we call His name every moment that we see, another miracle given to you or me, it truly won't be hard to praise Him evermore for those gifts I never truly thanked Him for.

—

God doesn't say, "Praise me, praise me, praise me," because He needs to hear the praise; *it's because in recognizing the gifts, it changes us. It changes the way we see things. It changes our gratitude function. He doesn't need the validation, He needs me, in the thanking, to go,"Oh, oh my heavens, there's another gift you gave me I missed. Thank you."*

———

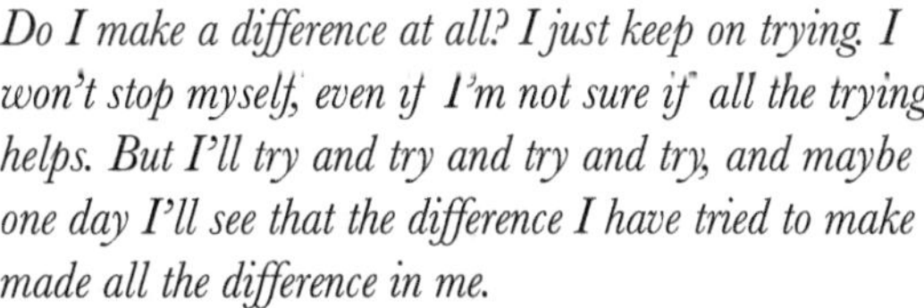

Do I make a difference at all? I just keep on trying. I won't stop myself, even if I'm not sure if all the trying helps. But I'll try and try and try and try, and maybe one day I'll see that the difference I have tried to make made all the difference in me.

———

I was going through such a hard time. It was a nine-year drought of thinking, *"Why won't he talk to me?"* And I remember thinking, if Jesus could go through that, and if Heavenly Father could say, "I have faith in Jesus," maybe your drought is your Father in Heaven saying, "Michael, *I have faith in you, that you will choose me even when you don't feel like I'm there.*

———

Writing the songs, thinking about the songs, and making up songs — that's how God talks to me. That's how I figure stuff out in my strange brain. And it may not be true or doctrinal or perfect, *but it's perfect for me.*

—

I'm so grateful that President Nelson said, "Hear Him." You know how profound that is to a songwriter? "Hear Him." Hear Him in the language and in the hope and in the melodies. You'll find a way to hear Him. *And the harder I try to listen, the more I realize He has a melody for every soul. He has a brilliant insight for every academician.* He has a perfect quote from a scripture to those who studied the scriptures, and He is in all of it — all of it. And my praise, my new song of praise, is, "Wow, another place you are in that I didn't know. That's my heart."

—

Song ~ The Light Will Come

The message of this moment is so clear. And as certain as the rising of the sun. If your world is filled with darkness, doubt or fear, just hold on, hold on, the light will come because everyone who's ever tried and failed, we stand much taller when the victory is won. And those who've been in darkness for a while, we kneel much longer when the light has come.

———

It's a lesson every one of us must learn, that the answers never come without a fight. And when it seems you've struggled far too long, just hold on, there will be light. Hold on. Hold on. The light will come. Hold on. If you feel trapped inside a never ending night, you just hold on. If you've forgotten how it feels to feel the light then hold on, if you are half crazy thinking maybe you're the only one who's afraid that light may never ever come. Just hold on. Hold on. The light will come. Hold on. Hold on. The light will come because you're not alone.

Even though right now you're on your own, you are loved in ways that can't be shown, your needs are known, but you're not alone. When you cry, you're just letting go of heartache deep inside. So tomorrow there'll be sunshine and sky and love close by, but you're not alone. And I know that it's not easy, and I know that it won't last because one who loves you more than me, He's sending His blessings fast. You're not alone. Say it one more time. I'm not alone. And even when it's hard, sometimes it's hard to find the words, your prayers are always heard. You're not alone. The lesson of this moment is clear. And as certain as the rising of the sun. If your world is filled with darkness, doubt or fear, just hold on, hold on, the light will come. The light will come.

—

Talk about God being great all the time — there are miracles. We don't see them, we don't know they're coming, *but they are real.*

—

You feel the abandonment because there are lessons you can't learn any other way. *He is in and all through things.* And the only voice in your head that says, "Well, you're not hearing it because you're not worthy," does not come from God. That comes from an adversary who wants to tell you you're not worthy — you're not good enough, it's not okay if you didn't get everything perfect. It is the voice that, right now in your heart, He speaks, as the scriptures are shared with you, that says, *"I am in it all with you. I am the light. The word, the light — that's me, and I'm not going anywhere."*

———

If He'll help *my* songs speak to somebody, *He'll touch anybody who's willing to put the stones out there, I think.* If He'll touch your podcast, to have it reach all the people it reaches and goes beyond, *He can help the guy that's sitting there right now,* listening to this saying, "Oh, but He's not going to touch mine."

———

Song ~One of the Ninety and Nine ♪

I am one of the 90 and nine. I'm not perfect, but basi-cally I'm doing fine, I have not lost my way. And I'm not going to stray. I'm just one of the 90 and nine. And I'm here in the heart of the fold. I'm not mindless, but I try to do like I'm told. I'm not tempted to run or become the lost one, I'm just here in the heart of the fold. So why is my shepherd coming this way towards me? He's holding his arms out and he's calling my name. Yes, he's calling my name.

—

♪ *How can this be? You see I'm just one of the 90 and nine. I've stumbled and fallen, but I've kept in line. I'm not one he must seek, I'm not that unique. I'm just one of the 90 and nine. So why is my shepherd treating me like a lost lamb? He's searching to find me and he's holding me now. Yes, he's holding me now. And he's teaching me who I am. So why am I feeling like I'm the only one here? It's like I'm his favorite, and he takes me aside, and he sweetly confides these remarkable words in my ear. He says, "You're one of the 90 and nine. Have you any idea how brightly you shine? You are safe in this fold and this time you were told," sorry, "that I know where you've been. So I know where you'll be because all your life you've been following me. You are more than just one of those sands of the sea or just one of the 90 at nine. No kids, you are mine. You are mine. You are mine. Yes, you're mine. Guess I'm one of the 90 and nine*

———

Proverbs 1-4; 15-16; 22; 31; Ecclesiastes 1-3; 11-12

Lincoln H. Blumell

> **Proverbs 3:5–7** *Trust in the Lord with all thine heart; and lean not unto thine own understanding. In all thy ways acknowledge him, and he shall direct thy paths. Be not wise in thine own eyes: fear the Lord, and depart from evil.*

In the big, big picture, *it's going to work out.* But, it may not work out here in this finite period of mortality, and you might not do things right. Again, generally, *people will be blessed.*

—

Really hard, terrible things, *they'll be for your good.* I can't help but think the Lord's thinking, "Well, with the eternal perspective that I have, these experiences will be for your good. They will bring you knowledge." Again, Proverbs is all about knowledge and wisdom; it's even used interchangeably: "You will have these experiences and you will understand."

—

If you take this bigger perspective, and you look at Ecclesiastes, *life is ephemeral. It's going to have an end. It's terminal. It's transitory.* Therefore, what is permanent? *Wisdom. We can carry knowledge out of this world.*

—

If I was going to give a theme to chapter one, it would be: *If you want to obtain wisdom, you're willing to be corrected; you're willing to be "chastised."* And there's a kind of discipline that goes with that.

——

If you really want to know something, it begins with the fear of the Lord. When I look at fear here, I wouldn't say we're terrified of the Lord. But, I might think of something like *reverence — acknowledging that there is a source beyond us for which we can draw on for knowledge and power — and then start with that.*

——

What is this path to wisdom like? In verse four it says, "If thou seekest her as silver and search for her as for hid treasure," then verse five, "thou shall understand the fear of the Lord and find the knowledge of God." *It requires seeking, and searching. In other words, it requires work.*

——

Yes, we have to have the cares of the world and go through a routine and do what we need to do: provide for ourselves, our families, all those things. *But are we doing eternally what's of most importance?*

—

What I would take, looking at this book in a positive light, especially in light of the epilogue, is, *keep your trust in the Lord. He's permanent. He's not fleeting,* but this life is ephemeral.

—

When I think about humility, I think of the word "meek." One of the meanings of meekness is lowly, but the root meaning is *fashionable.* And what it means by fashionable is you can actually fashion it, meaning, *you can mold it. That's a sense of meekness. It can still be molded. If you're meek, you can be worked with. You don't break.*

—

When you're chastised by the Lord, it's not a sign that He doesn't love you, as in verse 12; *it's the very opposite.*

—

Think about it. God says, "Go to earth and have this mortal experience. You're going to learn a lot and get a lot of wisdom, but it's going to be a lot of grief. You'll get a lot of joy, but it's going to be a hard process." And I think He's saying this, in a way: *"In life you'll grow, but it's hard. More wisdom isn't just a wonderful thing; it comes with pain and suffering and at a cost."*

—

It's amazing knowing that even in really hard things, you can trust in God. Keep the commandments. You don't know where your journey's going to go at times. Look forward, yet move forward with faith. I've had these experiences where I know God's there watching and helping me. And for me that really trumps anything else.

—

Isaiah 1-12

Jason Combs

> ***Isaiah 1:18*** *Come now, and let us reason together, saith the Lord: though your sins be as scarlet, they shall be as white as snow; though they be red like crimson, they shall be as wool.*

Because we're used to reading the Book of Mormon more than any other scripture, *we expect to find unique meaning in every sentence, and that's not true with Isaiah. Isaiah is painting a picture for us.* Everything we've read is just trying to help us to see that Israel is rebellious; that's his whole point. But he's taken a lot of words, a lot of poetic imagery, to say that.

———

If you are starting into Isaiah for the first time and you read a verse and you don't understand it, *that's okay.* Try reading the next verse or the verse after that, because *he's going to be repeating it.*

———

Sometimes we make Isaiah harder for ourselves by looking in every verse for the future prophecy, asking, "What is this foretelling here?" rather than, *"What is his message about how I should live faithfully?"*

———

Imagine us attending General Conference and listening to every word every prophet and apostle says, trying to find the secret clue in what they're saying about what's going to happen right before the second coming of Jesus. Well, most of what they're saying is not about the second coming of Jesus. Most of what they're saying is the message we need to hear in our present — in our here and now. And their message is about faith, about repentance, and about redemption. And, believe it or not, *Isaiah's messages are roughly the same — they're about faith, they're about repentance, they're about redemption.*

———

A speed read is not diligent. We need to search these things diligently, *for great are the words of Isaiah.*

———

I love the connection Mark Ellison made with the sacrament: "The sacrament itself can be a transformative power in our lives as we participate in that ordinance sincerely with the attitude Isaiah has of, "Here am I, send me," and of recognizing his own unworthiness, his own lack of preparation, and being open to the Lord to transform him to make him ready for that.

—

If there's anything that I want our listeners to know, it would be that *you can understand Isaiah. It is possible. You can do it.* So do it — read Isaiah. When you do, read it for its beauty, its poetry. *Read it for its witness to God's work among His people. Read Isaiah for what it meant in Isaiah's time and read Isaiah for what it means to you today.*

—

Jesus fulfills this call as God's Son in a way that Israel never could, and He does it for Israel. All of the covenant promises that God made with Israel are fulfilled in the ministry of Jesus Christ.

———

Our temple work is part of binding up peoples across dispensations in preparation for the second coming of Jesus Christ. The scattering was influencing the nation.

———

I think in the moments of our trials, we feel that need to cry out, *"Lord, how long?"* It can seem as if the trials will never end. And yet, the beautiful promise here is that *there will come a time when we will look back on those trials and they will seem but a moment, and we will be healed.* We will be able to sing to God, "Thou comfortedst me."

———

So, out of my conversion grew this love of
learning. I just fell in love with understanding
the scriptures on their terms as well as understanding how they apply to me today. So, there
have been challenging times over my learning, but they have tended to be those where I
allowed my studies to crowd out my faith or
treat religion as something separate from me.
I like what Elder Neal A. Maxwell said about
the disciple scholar eventually realizing they are
only a disciple. I am not two separate people, I
am one person who loves to study the scriptures
and learn from them from a historical perspective and finds great joy in how that informs my
faith. I also study scriptures to hear the word
of the Lord and open myself up to have His
promptings in my life.

———

Isaiah 13-35

Kerry Muhlestein

Isaiah 28:16 *Therefore thus saith the Lord God, Behold, I lay in Zion for a foundation a stone, a tried stone, a precious corner stone, a sure foundation: he that believeth shall not make haste.*

I know this seems strange to people, but for me, no book of scripture conveys the mercy of God like the Old Testament does. And it's because no matter how many times the people mess up, *He keeps giving them a chance.*

—

I try to liken myself to Israel as a whole, thinking that Israel messed up countless times and God is going to keep working with them even if it takes 2,500 years. Therefore, it might take 2,500 years for me, but if it takes 2,500 years, *fine. That's good with God. He'll be as patient as He needs to be with me.* As a covenant individual, that's comforting.

—

Satan really thinks he's big and bad, but the day is coming where he is just gone. And *the only thing that's going to last are things that are connected with God.*

—

The Old Testament teaches us about God's mercy more than any other book because we keep seeing how often His covenant people break the covenant and how He always gives them another chance. No matter how hard it is, no matter how much work it takes or how long it takes, *God always gives them another chance, and He will succeed in bringing them back. And that's incredible mercy.*

———

That's the message that Isaiah is trying to get to Ahaz, Hezekiah, and everyone who would ever listen to him: *start trusting in God. Forget about what the world is teaching you, and trust in God.*

———

In fact, I would say covenant and redemption are the two most prevalent themes in the Book of Isaiah. And of course, redemption comes because of God's servant who is primarily Christ, but also other servants. *But Christ primarily is the servant that gives us redemption.*

———

And I think we can all take a moment right now and ask ourselves, "What is it that I'm spending so much of my time and energy on, because the world has told me that this is important and I really should be putting my time and resources into something else." There's got to be some way for all of us that that's happening right now. *It's not an "if" question, it is a "how" question: How is it happening for us?*

—

These chapters, 24 through 27, they're sometimes called the little apocalypse because they're about this idea that "bad things will happen to you, but don't worry, *God will relieve the oppression and you'll be delivered and have joy.*

—

As bad as it is, eventually it gets good.

—

Christ is a divine warrior, He will destroy all oppression so that He can wipe our tears away.

—

"We have waited for Him, and He will save us. This is the Lord. We have waited for him. We will be glad and rejoice in His salvation." There are beautiful images of how all oppression, every kind of oppression, will end and God will save us and wipe away our tears.

—

There are Assyrians all over in our life. It might be pornography, or it might be depression and/or anxiety. It might be that I'm never going to get married, or it might be physical things that are afflicting us. Whatever it is, we all have an Assyrian in our life. *But what we can be sure of is that Christ can conquer every single one of those because He has a sword that is sore and great and strong. And after He conquers those oppressions, then He can wipe our tears away.*

—

As I struggle with things, *I rejoice in knowing that Jehovah has a sword. And one day that sword will conquer and lay waste to everything that is hard, and then He'll just turn around and wipe my tears away.*

—

When we are steeped in what the world is telling us, the things the prophets say don't make sense. We say, "You're wrong," and, "No, I can't believe you just said that." It *just doesn't compute for someone who is full of the spewing spiritual vomit of the world. But to those who are prepared, they say, "Oh, wait. I get what you're saying."* If people are even more prepared, they get even more. And we go bit by bit, line by line, precept upon precept. *And we go backward the same way when we're not prepared.*

—

If you look for that theme in Isaiah — the theme of God sending servants to help us be redeemed, and that He will never stop working with us until we are redeemed, and that when we receive that redemption, we will receive joy — if you look for that theme, you'll find it all over in Isaiah. There is more about praising and joy in Isaiah than I would've guessed before I started studying, but it's all over the place. There's also plenty of warning of consequences. If you don't repent, there's plenty about joy, but it's the joy of the redeemed, as we read here, because we wait. We waited on Christ because we kept the covenant. So, we did what we needed to and then that redemption came, bringing joy.

—

Isaiah 40-49

Terry Ball

> ***Isaiah 49:15*** *Can a woman forget her sucking child, that she should not have compassion on the son of her womb? Yea, they may forget, yet will I not forget thee.*

The last 27 chapters of Isaiah, starting with chapter 40, are really prophecies of *redemption and the greatness of God, and His plan and ability to save you.*

—

He is omnipotent, omniscient, omnipresent, and omnibenevolent. What a blessing it is to know that God has the *power* and the *knowledge* and the *presence* and the *love to save us.*

—

In chapter 41, you see that *God can deliver, He can choose, He can strengthen, He can help, He can uphold, He can defend, He can lead, He can protect, He can nourish, He can nurture, He can provide, and He can prophesy.* All of those things are verbs that God does. And in contrast, the idols in chapter 41 cannot create, they cannot move, they cannot act, they cannot choose, they cannot prophesy. *Jehovah can and will do all of these wonderful things for you, and idols can do nothing.*

—

They're going through all these acts of putting all their confidence in something that's not going to satiate their real needs. I always like to ask my students, *"So what are some modern-day ashes that people feed upon?"*

—

He does a marvelous job here of explaining how *Jehovah is a God.* He doesn't have to be made. Jehovah is a God who can choose, He doesn't have to be chosen. Jehovah's a God who loves you, it's not a one-way relationship. You can love Him, and He can return your love.

—

It's important to know *that He can create. He doesn't need to be created.*

—

It's not the law that saves, it is *redemption* that comes *because of Christ.*

—

We can become like our Father in Heaven. God's work and glory really is to bring to pass our immortality and eternal life. *Man and God are the same species. In fact, the whole purpose for our creation is to become like our Father in Heaven.*

—

God has a plan. In the last days, He's going to raise up a covenant people out of the Gentiles who will gather these scattered covenant people and witness that God is still working to save His children. They will be stewards of the covenant and prepare the world for the coming of Christ.

—

I love the assurance that chapter 49 gives you to know that *you're going to be a winner in the end.*

—

There is a certain confidence that comes from keeping the commandments, and a certain peace, that can't be found in any other way — even when things are going wrong.

—

The idea is as you partake of the water that I give you, not only is your thirst satiated, *but you become a source of water as well. I'm the fount of living water. You partake of what I have to give you, and you become a source of living water.*

—

One of the most distinguishing features of becoming like our Father in Heaven is that we have eternal seed, or *eternal increase.* This is one place from the scriptures that we can teach this idea about man's potential to become like God. If we hearken unto His commandments, then we become like Him unto our perfection. Our righteousness, our wholeness, our completeness, is continuous forever. It flows like a river and the waves of the sea, and we have eternal increase, seed as numerous as the sands of the sea.

—

There are a lot of hard questions out there that can challenge your faith. If you follow Elder Scott's example, you *let your faith inform the question,* and you come up with answers that feel right and are right. If you let the question inform your faith, you end up in the wrong place.

—

In a lot of ways, *faith really is a choice.* If you choose to believe, you can find so much that informs and affirms your faith. If you choose not to believe, there's lots of people who give you reasons not to believe.

—

There are rare people who appreciate the refining. *God's so good at making sure we have the experiences that are necessary to refine us.*

—

The truth is that faith supports truth and truth supports faith. My studies have informed my faith, and my faith has informed my studies; they go hand in hand. It's not surprising to me. It's only natural that the more education you get, the more you're going to understand and appreciate the truths that the gospel brings.

———

I don't think you need to know Hebrew to come to love this prophet. I don't think you need to be a biblical scholar. *You just have to have a heart that wants to know, love God, and spend the time with the text.*

———

I think Isaiah and our Heavenly Father are pleased when we read a passage and think about, "How does this apply to us?"

———

I don't think there's anything more important to serious scripture study than disciplining yourself to pondering. I define pondering as the act of asking questions and then looking, thinking about the answers. Something wonderful happens when you read a passage and ask, "How would I say this in my own words? What would I teach my children out of this? What could this mean to me? How was it fulfilled anciently? How does it apply to us today?" When you start to ask those questions, then you start to get feelings that enter your heart and thoughts that pop into your mind. It becomes this delicious discovery . . . an "aha experience," rather than the "ho- hum, I've got to trudge through this," and that can happen. It's disciplining yourself to search diligently, taking time to ponder, and the love grows.

———

Isaiah 50-57

Jennifer Platt

Isaiah 53:10 *Yet it pleased the Lord to bruise him; he hath put him to grief: when thou shalt make his soul an offering for sin, he shall see his seed, he shall prolong his days, and the pleasure of the Lord shall prosper in his hand.*

The sweetness of Isaiah is *in the slow.* So don't feel frustrated by the number of chapters, and be satisfied to just take a couple of verses. Take it slow, and read it out loud.

—

As much as we want to know the context of Isaiah and his time, *we need to know our context* and to be able to say: Here we are in the latter days, this is it. *And what am I doing to fulfill these prophecies? What am I doing to be a big player in this gathering that's being taught about here? Do I know what we're being invited to do? And am I getting really clear in the way I'm living my life?*

—

That's what Isaiah is bringing to us today — *Jesus, straightforward.* I want to be so clear that that's our objective, *it's Him,* and that the Holy Ghost will minister to us. *He's going to deliver that to our hearts.* We'll each recognize it in our own unique ways. Be still in that, and know that we are experiencing the Savior and His work.

—

Okay, we've got scattered Israel, and we're going to need something to piece this together. *Jesus, we need Jesus.*

——

That's such a great metaphor for understanding the scattering and the gathering — that God's family is fractured, and that *only through Jesus Christ can the family be brought back together and redeemed.*

——

What do I need to learn, and how can I better glorify the name of God?

——

Isaiah tells us the gathering is when we come to the knowledge of the Redeemer. So we've got to articulate, what does knowledge of Christ really mean? We need to be able to say, "Okay, I want to be gathered. *I need to know Him.*" And I think that knowing connotes an intimacy, a closeness, and a familiarity.

——

The gathering is knowing Christ, but it's not enough to know Him. And I think that a lot of times we want there to be a social Jesus where we need to know a doctrinal Jesus. Knowing Him is knowing, yes, His love, but also His law, and that will include entering into covenants and living covenants.

—

God wants us back. He wants to exalt us. Jesus is the way, through salvation, and the family is the context.

—

The covenant is always intact. He wants us back; it's the work of exaltation. He's very interested in us becoming gods.

—

There needs to be continuous learning of Him in order to become like Him.

—

It's this idea that every single day, *I need to be regathered. I need to regroup and ask, "Where am I?"* I need to redecide everyday I'm all in, covenant-living, and I want to become a god, and then remember that He will and He can cause me to become one.

—

It is important to see that it is in the service that we become. And we see it in Isaiah 53: *To be broken, to be malleable, to be taken to the dust, and that He'll exalt and lift, but that it is in His work we become.*

—

When do we start preparing for the sacrament? The moment it is finished. The moment we finish, we're preparing again for that next time to get to renew and remember. And that thinking about Him, that blessing to always have His spirit, if we will remember Him, *that's to be taken at face value. And that power is every one of ours, if we'll claim it, to be able to be strong like that.*

—

I do think sometimes we forget the purpose of a fallen state, *that we're meant to struggle, we're meant to become gods, and that there's going to be a lot of work to get there.*

———

Do you ever wonder about the covenant path? I love that visual. I love the language of it. Sometimes I hear people talking about it though, and they describe an ordinance path. We want to delineate it, make it a checklist. Like, "I was baptized, I received the Holy Ghost, the priesthood, and the temple and different things." *The reality of the covenant path is that it's work, and, in a lot of ways, we're cleaning up a path.* I mean, can you imagine, sometimes you see people on the side of the road with their vests on and they're cleaning up the road. *The covenant path is more about engagement. It's about living the covenants. It's more about practicing and becoming than it is about a delineated process,* and there's a messiness in that because it necessitates engagement with other people.

———

I think a lot of times we talk about Zion and we just can't wait for Jesus to come and clean this mess up, *forgetting that we've got work to do in building and establishing that.* And then He's going to come and help and be a part of it, *but He's already very much present in our lives.*

———

I wonder what it would look like for us to really live our covenants, the idea of "awake and awake, put on thy strength." *We live so beneath our privilege as covenant members of the Church of Jesus Christ,* and there's such power that we have to harness and claim.

———

I fear that we have such misunderstandings about the doctrine and gift of repentance. *It's not punishment but liberation,* and it is a chance to be expanded and to grow.

———

My experience has been, *He's never left me on my own. It's never been that life was always smooth sailing, but I know you're happier when you're living your covenants.* And there needs to be a really concerted, focused, intentional effort that I want to live my covenants today. *I want to have a straightforward experience with Jesus Christ. I want to draw Him into my life.*

—

Sure, there's a wrestle. We're mortal, and we're fallen, and there are conditions in a fallen state. But if we can tap back into our true identity, "I am a beloved daughter of God. I belong to the house of Israel," it will change our lives. Every night as we finish up family prayer with our kids, we say the family cheer: "I am loved. I belong to a family that loves me. I am a child of God." *I want my kids to know that deep.* I want them to know that it's going to govern who they are and how they're going to live.

—

Get engaged in what really matters: the work of salvation and the work of exaltation.

—

Isaiah is powerful in the way he draws us into the narrative, and we start to see that pronoun shift of *"we"* and *"our."* Like, *"We* hid, as it were, *our* faces from Him. We esteemed Him not. He was wounded for *our* transgressions, bruised for *our* iniquities. The chastisement of *our* peace was upon him. With His stripes, *we* are healed. *We,* like sheep, have gone astray."

—

A lot of times, we have an expectation for who He is and what He should be. And this is who He is: He is one who *redeems* and *saves,* and He wants us to partner in it. *He wants us to be a part of it.*

—

You get to choose. He says, "Walk with me and this is all yours, or walk on your own."

—

The Creator of all is going to be our great protector. He's going to protect, He's going to keep His promises, He's going to provide and preside. I mean, there's a proclamation for you. *He's going to take care of us as the great, ultimate husband that verse five calls him to be.*

—

There are so many among us that feel like they don't belong, or that their circumstances, life conditions, or frailties are such that there's not a place for them. But this, to me, *is God's evidence that everyone is invited. Everyone is invited to come if you'll just please keep Jesus as your focus. That no matter what, if He is your priority and your focus, and you're striving, the salvation and exaltation will work out on the other side.*

—

I'm so moved by this inclusion, but that inclusion isn't about staying as you are. You get to become, you get to act, and you get to do and progress.

———

I've been very blessed. It led me to choose an extraordinary companion. When you talk about "my kindness shall not depart from thee," I have it in the flesh. God sent and orchestrated a marriage to the kindest, purest of souls. To have a companion to complement and walk a parallel path of goodness together has been amazing for the last 10 years. I hope I can be a picture of hope — that there is hope — and that we can also say, "But if not, I know God knows us and that He wants us to become like Him." I try to remember that. I think that, for me, this is really helping my salvation and exaltation. I want to be like Them and progress. I love Jesus. I love Jesus Christ. That's how you make it. That's the only way to make it.

———

Finding Jesus Christ in the Old Testament

Isaiah 58-66

Ross D. Baron

> ***Isaiah 59:19*** *So shall they fear the name of the Lord from the west, and his glory from the rising of the sun. When the enemy shall come in like a flood, the Spirit of the Lord shall lift up a standard against him.*

The single most-important thing is that when you read Isaiah, *you're going to learn more about Jesus Christ. You can learn about His nature, His character, His attributes, and His perfections. We can learn about the plan.*

—

You can understand Isaiah. Now, you do have to pay a price for the nuggets and the treasures, and I would even say the peace and the power of the Spirit. But, if you would take that time to understand, Isaiah can be a conduit through which you can hear Him.

—

If I want the full blessing, *I've got to be fully obedient. If we want Isaiah 58 blessings, we've got to do Isaiah 58 obedience.*

—

Your connection with God is directly related to how you take care of the needy.

———

I had a kid in my class recently say, "You do you," and I 100% disagree with that. *I don't want to do me. I'm lame. I'm fallen. I want to do what Jesus wants me to do.* That's what I want to do, because I could be wrong. I'm pretty lousy at knowing exactly what I need and what I want. *I want what God wants for me; in fact, that's why I'm a member. That's why I'm in covenants, because I want what God wants.* I want prophetic direction. I want ordinances and covenants; I want that. *I want to choose the way of God. Even the Savior, the ultimate example, had to bend. He didn't want to do Him, He wanted to do the will of the Father.*

———

You must get a witness by the power of the
Holy Ghost and settle it in your heart. I am
settled in my heart. I love the Lord. I always tell
my students, "Look, you can ask me any question in class. But know one thing: I'm under the
umbrella of faith." I always tell them, "In my
class, we will study philosophy. You will know
as much as anybody about Kant or Aristotle or
Schopenhauer, whoever we're studying. But we
will do this. We will judge the philosophers by
the gospel, not the gospel by the philosophers.
Are we clear? We're never going to judge the
gospel by Aristotle, but we're going to judge Aristotle by the gospel. We're not going to dimin-
ish our rigor. But at the end of the day, what
the gospel of Jesus Christ teaches us trumps all
those other things."

———

Jeremiah 1-20

John Hilton III

> ***Jeremiah 18:6*** *O house of Israel, cannot I do with you as this potter? saith the Lord. Behold, as the clay is in the potter's hand, so are ye in mine hand, O house of Israel.*

All of us are going to backslide. We're all going to fall back into temptation at times. But the Lord is saying, *"I'm merciful. Come, return to me. We can make things work,"* and I love that.

———

Sometimes we're going to fail. *Just because we're working hard and doing what God wants us to do, it doesn't mean everything's going to turn out perfectly.*

———

I love that God has a plan for you. And back in Jeremiah chapter one verse five, the Lord says, "Before I formed you in the belly, I knew you." *We're not in a short-term relationship with the Lord; He's known us from the beginning, and I love that He's got a plan for us.* He's got hopes and dreams and a future with hope for you and for me, and I know that we can tap into that plan.

———

I love how they're able to still have hope in things that may not even happen in their life-time, that did not happen in their lifetime. And so to me, there's a clear message. *Maybe there's some problem in my life right now that actually is not going to be resolved in mortality. But Jacob, Nephi, and Jeremiah, they're having hope for future events. If I can have that eternal perspective, that's a game changer.*

———

I think it's fair to say that even if you're not a full-time missionary, *all of us are part of this.* We are all right now on the mission to be fishers, hunters, and gatherers, whether we've got a name badge or not.

———

In so many areas of our lives, I think it's easy to look sideways to see what other people are doing, to trust in the opinions of experts rather than really look upward to trust in God and in His prophets.

———

Maybe sometimes I feel like a misshapen piece of clay, and it's like, "Well, I'm useless." And God is saying, "No, no, no, don't worry. I can reshape you. You are clay in my hands." To me, that is a real message of hope, *that God is going to be able to shape me to do whatever it is He needs from me.*

———

We've been reading about the LORD, all caps, Jehovah, interacting with Jeremiah. And so, I would just want us to remember that Jesus Christ, He is the God of Abraham, Isaac, and Jacob. *And as we're reading about these interactions between Jeremiah and the Lord, these are interactions between Jeremiah and Jesus Christ, and they're helping us get to know Jesus Christ better.*

———

God has special plans for each of us, not just Jeremiah.

———

[After studying], I hope we have a little more of that "fire in the bones" ourselves, that God's word is burning in us; and it gets us excited to go back and explore other books of scripture. Let's get excited, and there's excitement, joy, and spiritual power in these amazing lesser-known books of the Bible. And so, I want us to remember that Jesus Christ is the God of Abraham, Isaac, and Jacob. And as we're reading about these interactions between Jeremiah and the Lord, these are interactions between Jeremiah and Jesus Christ, and they're helping us, I think, get to know Jesus Christ better. And more than anything else, I would hope that as a result of these episodes, we feel a greater connection with our Savior, Jesus Christ, and want to become more like Him.

———

Jeremiah 30-36

Michael Wilcox

> ***Jeremiah 31:3*** *The Lord hath appeared of old unto me, saying, Yea, I have loved thee with an everlasting love: therefore with lovingkindness have I drawn thee.*

Since they're going to be carried away captive, *you have to have hope.* Always, the Old Testament prophets have hope; *they always give hope. There is forgiveness, as the lesson title is, the mourning will be turned to joy.*

———

Old eyes see best. They're experienced. And as young people whose eyesight may not always be as good, we do call prophets "seers." *They're seers. They see things.*

———

We all come to Jesus. I go to him every day and say, "Master, if thou wilt, thou can make me clean." And He, filled with compassion, touches us all and says, "I will. Be thou clean." There is a balm in Gilead; *it's mercy, it is forgiveness, it is compassion.* And there is a physician there. *If my health is not recovered, it's because I've not availed myself of that physician and that healing.*

———

He knows where the verses are that we need, and if we'll be as familiar as we can, He can direct us in His own way. And then the words of verse 13 *will be true for all of us:* Whatever we face, "I will turn their mourning into joy and will comfort them and make them rejoice from their sorrow. And my people shall be satisfied with my goodness."

———

The Branch is going to plead the causes of our soul. The Branch's mercies are renewed every morning, so don't lament too deeply, Jeremiah says to us. *Don't stay in a state of sorrow, because there's always hope in something.*

———

The idea is that prophets are *always ahead of the times.* Prophets never go with the times — not because they're behind the times, as a lot of people want to think they are, *but because they're ahead of the times. They are seers.*

———

If God can find an excuse to honor us and bless us, *He will.*

———

Today you will find false prophets in the media, politics, activists, conspiracy theorists, celebrities, and experts. There are good political leaders and activists, and there's positive things, *but we have to be just a little bit careful.*

———

We have to learn to live with a bit of ambiguity and paradox. All of our lives have that mixture. *There is sorrow, but there is always hope.*

———

Prophets don't always have all the answers. Prophets themselves have questions; they wrestle just like we do. *They're doing the best they can. They question God too.*

—

The face of God that the Jews and the Old Testament gives us is *a god you can talk to, you can engage with. He's a very human god,* and you sense that in the prophets — this ability to engage God in conversation when you don't understand everything.

—

It's very powerful to really realize *God loves us.* Isaiah says, "You are precious to me, and I have loved you."

—

For me personally, these verses say to me: I know the thoughts I think toward you, and they're thoughts of peace. And I'm going to give you your expected end. *You call on me and pray, and I'll listen. And you'll find me when you search for me with all your heart* — in Denver, or Frankfurt, or Taipei, or Rio de Janeiro — *wherever you are. If you look for me, you're going to find me.* My thoughts of you are thoughts of peace, and I'll give you what you want in the end." Because most of us don't want improper things; most of us want what will truly make us happy. *God will give them to us if we'll wait patiently, as Jeremiah said. Just wait patiently.*

—

Ezekiel

Jan J. Martin

> **Ezekiel 33:7** *So thou, O son of man, I have set thee a watchman unto the house of Israel; therefore thou shalt hear the word at my mouth, and warn them from me.*

The Lord teaches very clearly *that wickedness is never swept under the rug* for anybody. *Everybody eventually is going to get the consequences.*

—

The covenant is eternal. The covenant is going to last, but we have to have repentance and we have to have a repentant people to help us here.

—

There are lots of things that are hard to articulate. And the feeling and the awe are really evident, and sometimes you cannot express it with words, and we need to remember that. *You can't always share spiritual experiences adequately.*

—

The Lord is concerned about everybody and will send messengers to everybody, even small captive populations in the middle of nowhere. *You just have to really appreciate how interested God is in people.*

—

Any time you've gone and done the right thing in any capacity where you have stewardship, you always feel that confirming recognition that you did your bit. And whatever people choose to do after that is no longer up to you because you've taught them or whatever. But there's a really nice feeling of, "I did that, and I am not accountable for them now." And there's something powerful in that.

———

I think we learn here that God works with natural consequences the majority of the time. He doesn't need to come and punish people, because He just lets the law work. He just lets the consequences come, and they inevitably do because they're eternal laws and they just work. *So, it's hard to have people thinking negatively of God here when this is just about people's choices.* And they've been warned and they keep choosing, but you reap what you sow and that's what's happening.

———

Sometimes that happens in people's marriages, they can never let what you apologize for go or get past it. And so you're constantly being held hostage by a mistake that you've more than made right and more than moved on from. You can understand how frustrating that is. *We're being promised that the Lord is not that type of partner. He doesn't keep bringing up the past and holding it against us. He won't bring it up anymore because we made it right, and it doesn't need to be brought up anymore. How comforting is that?*

———

We all have good intentions, and we all have desires to do things, but part of what we are judged on isn't just our desires; it's our works. There's both of those factors there. And I'm really glad that we have all these professions of goodness and want to do these things, *but the proof is in the behavior, and we need to live and change. And as you're changing and you're acting them out, that's really who you are.*

———

Part of our need when we're studying the Old Testament is to understand the culture and the context *but not miss these really precious glimpses of the character of God.* Because sometimes we read about all these destructions and things and then come away with the wrong idea, *but God is not enjoying this.* He doesn't want these consequences, which is why He sent a prophet. Which is why He sent the warnings. Which is why He works so hard to make sure our prophets are adamant about the warnings that they give. *Because He doesn't want any of this to happen to us, but sometimes we have to learn the hard way.*

——

It's just funny to think about sometimes, how hard it is for us to get this message: *"When I do good things, good consequences come. And when I don't do good things, negative consequences come."* And the Lord just kind of walks you through that again, and you see the logic, the simplicity of choice, and accountability, and agency, and how we can function in that a little more healthily.

——

That's a real message of hope, that the Atonement is available. It encompasses all things, *and we can move past all things. We can be changed.*

———

We shouldn't be worrying about these worldly allies. We need to make *the Lord our ally.*

———

Well, what is the solution to having no hope? *Hear the word of the Lord,* and then the Lord can cause the breath to enter, and that vitality is restored.

———

When you need to be revitalized and you need some hope, look at our promises. *Keep focusing on the things the Lord has promised for the future.*

———

You have these spiritual experiences that are helping you recognize where the Lord's hand is in all of this and that none of this Bible translation was accidental. And that the Lord is behind it in motivating it. But on every level of it, I have found my testimony is strengthened by the detail, the small things, and the stuff that is just too organized and too well-planned to be coincidental. Even when circumstances didn't match what I was expecting, He had it covered. . . and He had me in His hands, and I was okay. So even those journeys have strengthened my testimony. I have a very strong testimony of God, and my education and personal experiences have confirmed Him as a reality for me.

—

Daniel 1-6

Lili De Hoyos Anderson

> **Daniel 3:17–18** *If it be so, our God whom we serve is able to deliver us from the burning fiery furnace, and he will deliver us out of thine hand, O king. But if not, be it known unto thee, O king, that we will not serve thy gods, nor worship the golden image which thou hast set up.*

Great losses can come because of somebody else's sin. This does happen, *but that does not prevent the Lord from magnifying us. Whatever somebody else takes away from us does not stop us from coming to the Lord, becoming His disciple, and having Him magnify who we are so that we can fulfill our purpose,* remembering that all things will be restored to us in the millennium.

———

We often confuse agency with freedom. That's a big mistake. They're not the same thing. I think that sometimes we have parents saying, "Well, I don't want to take away my kids' agencies." I'm like, you can't. That's a gift bestowed by God Himself. *You can't take away anybody's agency. No one could take away Daniel's agency. He was always able to choose God or not.* That's what agency is. It's not the same as unlimited freedom where you can go where you want to and do what you want to and have what you want; that's a whole different thing. Freedom is a negotiable commodity.

———

You could bury me in a stone box a mile deep, and *I can still choose to worship God or I can choose to reject him. Agency continues even in captivity, and that is the right.*

—

He takes lead and turns it into gold in our lives, if we let Him.

—

I just think that if we read and study these things, we get a better understanding of omnipotence and omniscience; *God sees all things as present and that God has all power. He works in the affairs of men to accomplish His purposes, with or without their knowledge.*

—

It all works out in the end, and nothing is lost to the righteous. If we persist in righteousness, *any losses are compensated for in abundance.*

—

Bad things happen to good people, and life is unfair, and the children suffer for the sins of the parents. This happens all the time on our planet. Thankfully, it doesn't happen in every case, but it certainly happens. *Nevertheless, God can consecrate all of it for our good. He can magnify us in our weakness and in our injuries.* He can help us on that path to healing, knowing that *ultimate healing and complete restoration is to come. This is a temporary situation in this life. If we let our losses become our entire vision, we miss the opportunity that God gives us to make something of our lives however they've been hurt.* You don't see bitterness in Daniel. You don't see bitterness in Shadrach, Meshach, and Abednego. They have incredible trust in God.

———

These gifts come and they're tying it into their obedience, which makes perfect sense. Because *God reveals His secrets to people who obey, people that He can trust.*

———

Petition the Lord for light, truth, and understanding when it's needed. God knows all will impart, as appropriate, for our circumstances. He knows when to give that information and when it's not the time.

—

Whether you know it or not, God is in charge.

—

God does reveal His secrets to the prophets. It is exciting when we see that happening and recognize the hand of the Lord is never halted. It's never halted by the affairs of men; He utilizes them.

—

He never gets it wrong. He's not guessing.

—

Remember when we pray that we're invited to include something along the lines of "all these things according to Thy will," *in an acknowledgement that God's will may not be the same as ours, and that His is superior to ours.* We can petition for blessings that we think would be good for us or our stewardships, our families, and our loved ones, *but there should be that at least internal, if not articulated, acknowledgement that God's ways are better.*

———

The Lord knows those things, and we don't. If we try to get things to go our way, and then we don't think God is God because we don't always get things our way, *we're missing out on this level of faith* as demonstrated by these three amazing men, who say, "We know He can save us from the furnace. *But if He doesn't, that doesn't change a thing in the way we believe in God and will worship only Him because that would be for a higher purpose than perhaps we can see at this point in time. But we know that it is the case because God never fails to do what's best for us.*"

———

Trust that His ways are a manifestation of His love that He doesn't always give us what we want, *and trust that He has a higher purpose and that all will be restored in the end again. To know who He is and know that I'm not going to end up on the short end of the stick if I trust God, that is a different level.*

———

But as we pray, if we can plumb the depths of our heart, of our soul and mind, and say, "Am I willing to submit to all things that the Father seeth fit to inflict upon me *with the trust that it is ultimately for my gain?" He would not do these things for any other purpose than love, for any other purpose than perfect charity, because He knows and sees everything and knows my customized curriculum. Am I able to trust at that level so that I truly can say, "Nevertheless, thy will be done"?*

———

That is the pattern for each of us to come to — that place where *we don't just trust when things work out the way we want, we trust when they don't.*

———

But as we get into these higher levels of faith, the Lord is telling us, *"Trust me. You do the work because that's what I've asked you to do in keeping your covenants and doing the work of this life. And trust that the blessings will come at the time and in the way that I know will most benefit you. It may not look like that to you, but you trust me."*

—

Most of us will not be called upon to die for our testimonies, *but are we living our testimonies day by day and seeking to yield our wills to the will of the Lord* and do things in His way, not in our way?

—

It is so important to God that we be able to do the right thing without reward, even in the face of an immediate consequence that's negative. We're really robbing our children if we only let them do the things that they enjoy and that they're naturally good at, or things that they find a reward in pretty quickly.

—

It really is in these day-by-day yieldings of our natural-man desires, in order to do things in God's way, that we progress in our lives. That's what builds the kind of trust that, if required, will lead to these kinds of sacrifices. *But whether or not it's required in this life, it is required that we build that trust in God and that we try not to carve out the blessings that we want and say, "If you really love me, Lord, this is what you'll do for me."*

———

Sometimes we see Him as kind of hands-off, and some people complain about that. Why won't God do this? Why won't God do that? *His ways are higher. He's playing the long game. He always plays the long game. It's about eternity. Trust in Him.* Even if you can't see exactly what His purpose is right now, you know His purposes are good, and they are bringing to pass the immortality and the eternal life of men. That's always the long game He's playing. Then, when we have eyes to see, we can see that *even the times He's hands off, it's for our good. We see His hand even when it is restrained.*

———

We're not going to become Zion people after Christ comes. *We need to become Zion people now.*

—

Too often, a lot of the pain in our life is because *we don't know who He is. We have our doubts about how merciful, or how good, or how trustworthy He is, and that is our failing because He is forever the same yesterday, today, and forever — all goodness, all love, perfect charity. We can trust it.* Is it a leap of faith? Absolutely. Faith is believing what we can't see. It's a choice to believe that. It's our choice in how we choose to see what happens in life. Do we take off our shoes because we see Him, and know who He is, and know His perfect character? Or do we go around with that chip on our shoulder that gets knocked off all the time because life is hard for the unbeliever? *It's hard for everybody.*

—

How do kids learn to respect deity? *Well, they start with the parent figures that they grow up with,* because as a little child that's what they know. If they learn to treat that parent with respect, it is not difficult to transfer that respect to a Heavenly Parent. *If they grow up without respect toward their earthly parents, why should they respect God who is just another parent after all?*

———

How a child has a relationship with their earthly parents *very much* impacts their openness and their approach to a relationship with a Heavenly Parent.

———

Now we are so blessed to have the gospel of Jesus Christ because we can know what's important and what's not. *If it matters to God, it should matter to us as parents. If it doesn't matter to God, we should drop it.*

———

Ultimately, *the product of parenting is the parent.* It's what we learn to do that makes us more like God, because He is an authoritative parent. Our children will exercise their agency to comply or to not comply. Nevertheless, we have been told that there is more likelihood that children will comply when parents know how to teach. *This helps us to grow in our roles as parents and to become more like God Himself. It gives our children the best possible chance. Then they make their own choices, and we don't blame the parents for that.*

——

Of course, we're not going to be 100% consistent, *but if we keep trying, and praying, and seeking revelation and guidance from the Spirit, and we are earnest in our endeavors to become a better version of ourselves as a parent, to learn more about God-like parenting, God will bless us.* He will bless and consecrate that experience for our good, and our children will be recipients of that better parenting, whatever they choose to do with it.

——

God doesn't really ask us to be our best. I mean, that's sort of a weird target. Some days, people can lift cars off children. If I'm not doing that every day, am I doing my best? *That's not really what God asks. What God asks repeatedly in scripture is that we be diligent. Diligence is the way to go forward.* Not worrying about perfection.

———

All receive more than we deserve. For those who want it, we can have all that the Father offers us. *We can be co-heirs with Christ.* That blows my mind. I don't know how to contain that idea — that *He can raise us to the stature of Christ Himself, our Savior and Redeemer, the Lamb of God.* I mean, it's amazing how generous this plan is. We suffer so much because we don't think of how merciful it is.

———

Again, God doesn't give us all the answers yet, *but He asks us to believe Him and that there will be joy.*

—

We cannot become bitter. We cannot fail in our faith because *God is good. He is loving and merciful. It never faileth. His goodness never faileth.* He wants us to be full of joy as He is, and we can start that right now if we trust in Him.

—

Trust God. We've been talking about that throughout this wonderful time with Daniel. We can, as parents, trust God when He says that keeping our covenants will be an outcome that is more wonderful than we can imagine with our finite, limited, mortal brains. We can trust Him.

—

Hosea, Joel

Aaron Schade

> ***Joel 2:13*** *And rend your heart, and not your garments, and turn unto the Lord your God: for he is gracious and merciful, slow to anger, and of great kindness, and repenteth him of the evil.*

Hosea is a book about love, it's about a relationship with God. It's about one that's *trying to get us to examine ourselves and our relationship with Him.* So if we can muscle past the first couple of verses and see them for what they're saying, we start to see that *this is a deep love story between us, ancient Israel, and by extension, our relationship to God.*

——

I'm not sure that Hosea is trying to get us to beat our head against the wall, trying to figure out what God is doing, but more to use this as a message to say, *"What are we as individuals and as people doing in our relationship to God?"*

——

How do we submit our thoughts, our feelings, and our desires to God in a way that is productive and fruitful for us to the point where *I can have it genuine change of who I am, not just in an outward appearance, but who I genuinely become.*

——

What is it that I see in my covenants with God? And *do I understand how much He actually loves and cares about me?*

———

The long game for God is "what can *grow* and be accomplished through all of this?"

———

Even though His physical presence may not be here now, *there will come a time where you experience His presence* and everything that comes with great or dreadful, *and that's going to be something that then becomes glorious.*

———

All of this concept of repentance is: *Please go back to God* and allow Him to show you the type of love that you've been craving through all of this, and that *He's never ever withdrawn.*

———

There's something about this concept of never ever forgetting all of the power that God has to enact in our lives, *and the love that He does it with.*

—

The message here is, *"No matter how hard things get, I will not forget you and I'm always here for you."*

—

Just because we're trying to do the best we can *doesn't spare us from loss. It doesn't mean we won't lose people that are close to us. It doesn't mean that life is going to be easy.* But the book is trying to get us to look at the big picture through the eyes of God, and try, and just, in some small measure, understand what He's trying to accomplish and that He's trying to draw us closer to Him. And whether that's in life or after death, *the hope is that eventually we'll have this reunification with God that would be something far beyond any peace or hope or happiness that we could ever find in any other source in life.*

—

If you want to sow a celestial life, you need to plant celestial seeds. Now, that doesn't mean that everybody's always going to like you if you treat people with love. It doesn't mean they're going to love you back, *but at least you're giving a chance for something to grow through all of that.* And again, seeds can grow in very different ways. Particularly, *learning to love somebody that doesn't love you back can be an extremely powerful lesson in life.*

———

God really does have mercy, *but you've got to come back to Him.*

———

God is very close to us and endearing to us in our lives if we let Him. And even if we don't let Him, *He'll keep trying.*

———

At some point each of us meets our Maker, and the question is, *are we prepared for that?*

———

Keeping a covenant doesn't mean a life free of adversity, but rather *there is hope in the future.*

—

And so again, it's kind of looking back and inviting us to think that all of those times we look at scripture and say, "Where was God in the people's lives then? Why did He let this happen?" *This was never about God losing a love for any of His children; it was about helping them through and loving them more through those difficult times.*

—

What lies on the other side of the next tragedy is God.

—

Eventually, God will come and make all things right that the world put wrong.

—

I didn't know it at the time, but "let God prevail" was something I was trying to do without even knowing it. We're always going to be presented with ideas that seem contradictory and ideas that seem like they may be a theological knot that we can't simply untie. But ultimately, I trust in an all-knowing, omniscient God who does know the answers to all these things. And I'm not going to let doubt trump what I know — His love and compassion. So, that's always been the anchor in my life that's only accentuated through my studies. In fact, it's given me a bit of humility, and that's something that has increased my appreciation and love for God. And so, that's been something that I've just always tried to make my guiding principle in life: to realize that though I don't have the answers, I know He does.

—

Amos, Obadiah

Ryan C. Davis

> ***Amos 4:13*** *For, lo, he that formeth the mountains, and createth the wind, and declareth unto man what is his thought, that maketh the morning darkness, and treadeth upon the high places of the earth, The Lord, The God of hosts, is his name.*

Amos begins to tell us that lion's roar for a reason. So if you hear a lion roaring, there's a reason He's roaring. This kind of sets us up to think, okay, *if God is the lion and He's roaring, then we need to wonder why.*

———

One of the themes of Amos is our relationship with God, *that God does things and it's our choice to respond.*

———

One of Amos' messages is about the core of what it means to be a disciple of Jesus Christ, *and it is to make people our focus. People are not a means to an end; people are the end themselves. That's what we're here to do, is to take care of people.*

———

Your relationship with those around you and your relationship with God *are very much connected.*

———

Jesus — He's the kid on the playground that saves us from the bully and then afterward says, *"Will you be my friend, and will you help me rescue other people?"* And that's, I think, really the foundation of what it means to have a covenant relationship with Jesus Christ — that our *Heavenly Father and Jesus Christ reach out to us in love and deliverance, and after they've rescued us, say. "Join with me."*

———

Don't wait for them to earn it. Don't wait for them to deserve it. *Just go and help them no matter what.*

———

I think sometimes we think, "Oh, I can live the gospel in my bedroom. I can read my scriptures, say my prayers, and do what I need to do." *But that's prelude to the work of salvation. The work of salvation is literally helping people and rescuing them out of hard times.*

———

Small children don't pad your bank account, they don't pay your mortgage, they don't help you sleep at night, they don't make your life less stressful. The question is, why do we spend our entire life loving and serving and taking care of these little ones? And the answer is *because we love them and it makes life meaningful and beautiful.* That's what life's about. And it's the same reason why God spends His life serving us and loving us and taking care of us, *even if we don't pay the mortgage,* if we're unprofitable servants, *because He loves us and we make His life meaningful and beautiful.*

—

One thing that's really struck me that I've learned from the Old Testament is the importance of relationships. *That it's their relationship with God that should inform what their relationship with those around them is about.* And that relationship with God begins with love. It begins with taking care of someone *because they need help. And that's how we need to relate with those around us.*

—

Really, the only thing that you can take with you into the next life are your relationships. *That's why we go to the temple.* We make relationships with God through covenants and we make relationships with our family members.

———

For God to be someone who is righteous means that *He wants to rescue you* and get you out of every situation that is difficult and where you are suffering. *That's why God is righteous.*

———

That word "perfect" means complete. And I think one of the ways to read this is that *we need to be complete in our love.* Not partial, but love all people all the time.

———

The reason Jesus says "blessed are you, if you hunger and you thirst after righteousness" is because *this is what the covenant people of the Lord are here to do for the world.* We're here to find those that are hungering and thirsting, and give it to them *through our friendship, through our love, through our service, and being there for them as they need it.* If you're hungry, we'll feed you. If you're naked, we'll clothe you. If you are sick, we'll heal you — and these kinds of things. *This is what the covenant people of the Lord are here to do for the world.*

—

And that's what it means to be a disciple. It means *we've realized what God has done for us, and now we want to do good for others. We want to stand alongside Jesus in helping Him do good here in this world.*

—

If you're going through a tough time, *reach out to Him, He'll be there for you.*

———

One thing I like about that is repentance isn't just thinking, "I messed up, so what do I need to do differently?" Repentance is thinking, "What is going on in my family's life? How can I help them? What is going on in my neighbor's life? What can I do to be a part of the solution? What can I do to better work alongside Jesus Christ in lifting the children of God in this world?" Because *repentance isn't just turning away from something, it's putting something in its place. And what do we put in its place? We put righteousness there, and this is what righteousness is all about.*

———

If you don't listen to the Lord, *then you might stop hearing Him speak to you.*

———

When we think about a savior standing on Mount Zion, if we can think about that *as ourselves, as disciples of Christ* standing on Mount Zion, it's our mission to find those who suffer and to comfort them, *to bring them to the Lord,* to Mount Zion, where *they can be healed and taken care of.*

—

We don't have to go out of our way to be disciples of Christ. *The people that need us are there and are in our way.* We just need to open our eyes and realize that there are people that are hungering and thirsting for righteousness *right next to us.*

—

As I've learned more and more, I've had to
learn to be comfortable with not knowing
things. And I've realized that that's really what
faith is. My studies have given me an opportunity for faith. It's given texture to the scriptures,
which has helped me establish my relationship
with Jesus Christ and our Heavenly Father. And
that relationship is based on faith. Faith is trust.
I'm okay not having the answers to all my questions. But I know He's there, and I'm a disciple
of Jesus Christ, and I'm just excited to be on
His team and working next to Him to do good.
More than anything, my studies have helped
me realize that my relationship with my Heavenly Father and my Savior, Jesus Christ, really
matters in life. And that relationship will see me
through every difficulty. And I've learned from
Amos . . . that I have to do something for those
around me.

—

Jonah, Micah

Joshua Sears

Micah 7:19 He will turn again, he will have compassion upon us; he will subdue our iniquities; and thou wilt cast all their sins into the depths of the sea.

Whether Jonah in the belly of the whale or anybody in dire straits, the temple is where He goes. He knows that's where God's presence is and His mind is drawn to the temple. I think that is something we can really relate to.

———

The imagery here is powerful. You are down in those depths, you can't be saved, and then *Jehovah reaches down there and picks you up from those dark, watery depths and brings you back up to life.*

———

That covenant love and loyalty is up to us. *God is never going to forsake it,* but we can place ourselves outside of those blessings there if we choose to stray.

———

If the natural man is an enemy to God, that suggests that all of us are His enemies to some extent, and we are only saved through the Atonement of Christ the Lord.

———

Am I willing to forgive people who have done wrong? *Even if it's wrong to me?*

———

The Book of Jonah really is an invitation to ask the question, *are you putting limits on God's generosity, mercy, and grace?*

———

You have got to believe people can change and improve. *If we want God to be gracious and merciful with us, we have got to extend that to others.*

———

The Lord is promising eventual salvation for the remnant, but it doesn't mean there's not going to be a painful difficult road to get there before you get to that final restoration.

———

When you have deep spiritual questions, do you go unto the Lord in prayer? Do you listen to the prophets? Do you read the scriptures, or do you do the typical thing that anyone in the world would do: Google your deep spiritual questions, listen to podcasts from people who are antagonistic, listen to people who don't even believe in God and get their framework. Right? *Which way are you turning? That's something we all have to figure out, because we all have kind of these dual identities as members of a modern secular culture and as people who have covenanted in the Church to follow Jesus Christ.*

———

It doesn't matter if you're a literal descendant of Israel or if you're just adopted in, *the blessings are the same.* What matters in the end is covenant-keeping whatever your background is.

———

You don't have to go to these extremes like rivers of oil and thousands of sacrifices for God. He is like, "Look, all I want you to do is love me, be true to your covenants, and treat people right."

———

If someone's saying, "You know what? My life stinks. I'm surrounded by people I don't trust." Everything is just miserable. But what am I going to do about this? Am I going to give into despair? No. *I'm going to look to the Lord. He's going to hear me. When I'm in darkness, He'll be my light.*

———

He delights in extending that love and mercy and loyalty to us. It's not like He's grumbling about it. Like, "Oh man, you messed up again. Now I'm going to have to forgive you, I guess." No. He delights in it. He loves extending mercy. He loves forgiving. *This is what gets Him happy — being able to extend that kind of love and mercy to us.*

—

God wants you to do justly, treat people right, love Hesed, and walk humbly before God. "You be faithful, and loyal, and loving to me." And that's what Jesus was getting at. What are the two greatest commandments? Love God. Love your neighbor. I think the promise here of the prophets is *no, you or they are never so far gone* that the light of that love that He has, that stems from His covenant with us, can't reach us and them. *No matter how long it takes, no matter what He's gotten to do, He's never going to be unfaithful to that covenant and loyalty that He has. He'll reach out, He'll humble us if He needs to. He'll do whatever it takes* to call and plead. And as soon as we turn to Him, sincerely repenting and wanting to make that relationship whole again, *He will delight in forgetting all that happened and welcome us back as if it never happened* — hurling those sins into the sea to be forgotten forever.

———

Nahum, Habakkuk, Zephaniah

Joshua Matson

> ***Habakkuk 3:17–18*** *Although the fig tree shall not blossom, neither shall fruit be in the vines; the labour of the olive shall fail, and the fields shall yield no meat; the flock shall be cut off from the fold, and there shall be no herd in the stalls: Yet I will rejoice in the Lord, I will joy in the God of my salvation.*

For an ancient and modern audience who's reading Nahum, the first questions we can ask are, *"Are they talking about me?"* and, "What can I learn from this text as it relates to my situation and my standing and my relationship with God?"

———

When I'm reading Nahum, I can't help but think, "What's the ending of my story? Is my story going to be one of redemption and forgiveness? Or is my story going to be one of destruction and standing in opposition to God?"

———

How amazing is that for you and I as we study this text with the Holy Ghost and as we prayerfully seek to get insight, to be able to say, "God will reveal to me that meaning, and I'm not going to limit myself to someone else's interpretation of the text."

———

That last line that you read there, that "trust in him," the Hebrew actually better reads *"to those who seek refuge in Him."* So, it's not just that I trust God or I know God can do these things, but it's this intentionality of *finding refuge in God.* That's what is going to separate the righteous covenant people and those who are going to be destroyed, those who come to seek refuge from Him as opposed to finding refuge in other places. That's really the question of Nahum: Are you on the Lord's side or have you sided with others who are not seeking refuge in the Lord?

—

And so, there's an irony to the fact that people who had learned so well to manage water and to become a city that's renowned for its utilization of water *would then be destroyed by that very thing.* One scholar, he actually says the token of its strength is now a simile for its downfall. How often do sometimes we get puffed up in our own pride of who we are or what we are doing, and then it ultimately leads to our distancing ourselves from God and then our own downfall?

—

That's the beauty of these prophets — people don't study them because they are hard to understand, but sometimes the most beautiful things in life take effort to understand.

—

Nineveh put their trust in the wrong shepherd. And because of that, they were led astray. But we are disciples of the Good Shepherd, who if we find refuge in Him, we will be protected.

—

I love this idea that our relationship with God is a wrestle. *Sometimes we approach heaven too obliquely.* We say, "Oh, I can't get upset with God. I can't argue with God. I can't wrestle with God." And one thing that I like to tell my students all the time is, "Friends, I think God can handle it. If we're frustrated with God or if we don't understand something, I think God can handle it if we shake our fists sometimes and say, 'God, why can't I understand this?' or, 'Why are you doing this?'"

—

Habakkuk has just reached the point where
he looks and he goes, "God, are you just never
going to listen to me? Are you never going to
answer my prayers and the needs that I have in
my life?" I can't think of a more connective way
to see Habakkuk than to think of the millions
of people who've prayed the same prayer that
we see in Joseph, and in Habakkuk, and in
the Psalms.

———

Habakkuk starts with this indignation and says,
"No, why aren't you doing justice, God?" And
then he says, "Wait a second. That's not how I
would do it, but now I understand better that
your ways are better than my ways. And I am
willing to submit my will to your will. And I am
willing to understand that what you are doing
is with a grander perspective than what I would
do if I was in your shoes."

———

For us, it's easy to put distance between us and idols. We go, "Oh, I don't build an idol and put it in my bedroom or go to some temple." But in an essence, *this is anything that we put our trust in that's not God.* It may even be gold and silver, just not in the form of a small statue.

——

We can wrestle with the Lord, but when the Lord gives us an answer, *it's inappropriate for us to continue to rail and say God is not answering our prayers.* When we know that we've received an answer, it's time for us to keep silence before Him.

——

Habakkuk's wrestle turns into a song of jubilant praise and joy that what he learned is that God is actually fighting for justice and is listening to His people's prayers, and that we simply need to trust in Him and rejoice in Him so that we can have joy.

——

It's really encouraging that if I have struggles, if I think that God's not listening to my prayers, if I continue to wrestle, *I eventually will hear Him.*

—

If there's one thing that I've come to know more surely throughout my life, it's the fact that the Restoration of the gospel of Jesus Christ is a real event and that the restored gospel of Jesus Christ on the earth is a means by which God is bringing salvation to His children. I love the idea of being part of the gathering of Israel, there's no greater work in the world. I have seen how studying the Bible and becoming proficient in its languages and in the language of scholarship helps gather Israel. So, I get excited that gaining an education is encouraged by the Restoration, but it's also part of building the Restoration for all of God's children to come unto Him.

—

Haggai, Zechariah

Anthony Sweat

> **Zechariah 1:3** *Therefore say thou unto them, Thus saith the Lord of hosts; Turn ye unto me, saith the Lord of hosts, and I will turn unto you, saith the Lord of hosts.*

Where are our efforts? Where's our energy? Where are our priorities? Are they centered in the things that won't fill, and won't last, and aren't bringing true joy? *Or are they centered in the things in the temple?*

—

If I am spending all my time caring for my own home and building it up, making it nice — which there's nothing wrong with that, but if I'm omitting caring about the Lord's home and spending my time there — and I find wonderful things to decorate my home, can I make sure I'm finding names to take to the Lord's home? If we're not doing those things, the Lord might be saying to you and I, "Maybe we should reconsider our ways a little bit."

—

With some of the injustices, unfairnesses, or losses that we experience in mortality, *the Lord is a Restorer — that's one of His central titles.* He's a Restorer of lost blessings, of lost hope, through this fallen world, and He can make the future greater than the past.

———

The invitation here is: Do you want greater peace? Do you want greater rest? Do you want greater power to detect the deceptions of the adversary, to overcome the trials and tribulations of mortality, greater knowledge, greater ability to hear the voice of God, greater connection with the ministering of angels, greater ability to understand the Lord's ways? That's what the temple's offering us. That's what endowment is.

———

Endowment, as I've said before, is not a cere-mony. *Endowment is a power.* The ceremony or the presentation of the endowment that we participate in is an authorized ritual to open up and facilitate the power. The power of godliness is found in these ordinances, but we have to live our lives in such a way by adhering to these covenants and concepts in the temple that, line upon line and bit by bit, bring that into our life — this greater peace, this greater happiness, this greater knowledge, this greater rest, this greater connection to God.

———

Our job is to consider our ways compared to the Lord's ways, reevaluate, and realign. *That's really what repentance is at its heart — a simple realignment.* I actually think that invitation to consider our ways is a hopeful and loving thing; *it's not a condemnation.*

———

Sometimes in our own lives we — rightly so — want the Garden of Eden, and we want these different challenges to be taken out of our lives, our temporal lives. And Jesus is here to say, "I'm here to heal your soul. I'm here to redeem you from sin." And, it won't be until the millennium that we're completely redeemed from the temporal aspects of the fall. We need to make sure we don't get those out of whack and lose our faith in the work of the Messiah either.

——

It's undoubted to see this connection of a people who are not only preparing *a place* for the Savior, *but they're preparing themselves.* Zion can only be built on principles of righteousness, and the purpose of Zion is to gather people around the temple so they can know the Lord — they can know His ways, they can follow Him, and they can *be a people prepared to receive Him.*

——

The home is where we practice and try to learn to implement these holy ways of living, and it's because it's the best laboratory to figure them out together.

———

No matter where you're coming from, *there's always reason to have hope because of the Savior. His promises are sure.*

———

As we prepare ourselves to receive the Messiah for his second coming, like these people were trying to prepare themselves for his first coming, I just hope that nobody out there loses hope. I sometimes, in my position as a religion teacher, I see people who sometimes get a little frustrated or they find flaws and what they perceive to be weaknesses or missteps or fallen aspects of the restoration, answers we don't know, things that are unresolved. And sometimes, I just want to say to them, *have hope*. The arc of the world is bending toward restoration. *Just like how Jerusalem and the temple was restored here, the world is going to be restored.* Jesus will overcome all the effects of the fall of Adam and Eve. *He is a complete redeemer, from sin and death, but injustice also, unfairness, ignorance, pain, suffering. All the effects of the fall of Adam and Eve of this telestial mortal sphere will be conquered.* Think if the people of Haggai had lost their animus. Think if they had lost their hope, simply because they couldn't see it yet, and things were difficult and unknown and challenging. That's part of having faith and of continuing in the ongoing restoration is having hope that Jesus will fulfill these promises.

———

Malachi

Barbara Gardner

Malachi 4:5–6 *Behold I will send you Elijah the prophet before the coming of the great and dreadful day of the Lord: And he shall turn the heart of the fathers to the children, and the heart of the children to their fathers, lest I come and smite the earth with a curse.*

The Lord gives 100%, and He wants His covenant people to also give 100%. It's the reality of our life today. It is hard to give it all. These people are holding back a little bit. They have their favorite sins or they have ways of thinking that they can deceive the Lord, *but the Lord will not be deceived. And that's a hard thing for all of us.*

—

God has said to us, "Love me in two ways: Keep my commandments and feed my sheep." And these people are not willing to do either of those things, but yet, *they're wondering why God isn't showing His love to them. But in reality, He is;* they just can't see it because they're not willing to keep His commandments. *They're blind to reality because of their distrust and disobedience.*

—

None of us are perfect, and I think that's partially the struggle that each of us has. We all know that we have our favorite sins. We all know that we're holding back some things. I think the difference, though, is our intention to give it all to Christ — to become better through the Atonement of Jesus Christ — where in this case, it looks like they're making a mockery and they're intentionally trying to deceive. That's the distinction. And I think that's critical to say to ourselves, "Lord, is it I?" Am I holding back? Is there something wrong with me, or am I blaming and saying, "No actually I'm really good."

———

You may see temporarily that some people that are not being obedient are getting blessed, but in reality, *they will be my jewels. You who are obedient will be my jewels. You'll have everything that I have. You become heirs of all that I have.* Don't worry about complaining because you didn't get a nice car. You're going to have mansions.

———

If Satan is going to try to destroy one thing in our day and age at any time, it's what he wants more desperately than anything. And it's an eternal, united, oneness relationship that only our Heavenly Parents have with each other and with Their children. And Satan cannot have it. He chose to rebel. And of all the things that he wants to destroy, it's the family.

———

You're not going to get rich being a covenant keeper. Some people will, some people won't — but that's not the point. It's not that kind of richness. It's just like He says, and we already talked about it in chapter three, which is where He says, "I will make up my jewels." *We are the money to the Lord.* We are His great value. We are His glory. It's people. And that's the thing with tithing — it's not about the money, *it's about what God is creating. He's creating His jewels as we give up our jewels.*

———

When Satan wins, he seems to feel like he has more power. When our Heavenly Father wins, *we* have more power. And God wants to endow us with His power. He wants us to become like He is. He wants us to become eternal, heavenly parents.

—

The expectation wasn't that we would ever get rich — we never were. But the expectation from my father and my mother was if they paid their tithing, *the Lord would help us keep our covenants. And He always did.*

—

People live beyond the veil. *Death is a comma,* and they want to be found, and we are working together for their salvation. *Jesus Christ paid the price through His Atonement to make it so that we can have eternal families.*

—

God is God. He's able to perhaps have a different law than we are. But just like Him, I think we are taught *we just don't give up.* And there's not an age when, all of a sudden, we stop being parents. We love, we care, and we don't give up.

—

Our Father in Heaven, and Jesus Christ, wants so bad to just show us His love. Even with all of this wickedness, He's coming with the intention of helping them, even then, as a Purifier and as a Healer. But they have to want it. They have to be willing to be cleansed.

—

I love President Eyring and his talk where he was speaking to women specifically. He says, "My experience has taught me that Heavenly Father's daughters have a gift to allay contention and to promote righteousness with their love of God, and with the love of God, they engender in those they serve." For all of us together — women and men working together as we are creating Zion — to remember that this idea of priesthood and temple is women and men together, working together for the salvation of all of our Heavenly Parents' children . . . it's an exciting, fun, glorious work.

———

Christmas

Jeffrey Chadwick

> **Luke 2:7** *And she brought forth her firstborn son, and wrapped him in swaddling clothes, and laid him in a manger; because there was no room for them in the inn.*

The Hebrew word for ensign is actually "nes," which means a signal but is also the word for miracle. Therefore, it's a miraculous signal flag. The Lord will raise a miraculous signal flag, which will institute or initiate the gathering of Israel. And what is that? Well, of course, *it is the work of Christ and, in these latter days, it is the Restoration.*

—

What's it like to be a young woman, 17-ish in a traditional Jewish society in Nazareth, not married, but you're pregnant? *How in the world must this have been for Mary?*

—

Can you imagine how difficult it was for this young couple in a traditional society to be thought of by the whole village, even maybe by your parents, of having engaged in sexual re-lations and produced a child before your actual marriage date?

—

They are such great examples of taking the situation that's given to you, which is sometimes a difficult situation, and saying, *"We will now make the word of the Lord and the work of the Lord work."*

———

We've always painted Joseph and Mary, a young couple, as being victims of circumstance. Yeah, the circumstance was that the Son of God was going to be born, but it's not Roman soldiers or taxes that drove them to Bethlehem; *it is that they knew who this child was and they knew where it had to be born.*

———

Christmas is about the birth of Christ and the gift to us in the world, and that's what we should remember. *But the story itself is really the story of the faithfulness of Joseph and Mary, these two wonderful people who would raise the Messiah and Savior of the world.*

———

There was never a greater and more trusted servant of the Lord — all the prophets notwithstanding — than Joseph of Nazareth, whom God the Father would trust to raise His Son.

———

The angels said unto them, "Fear not. I bring you good tidings of great joy, which shall be to all people." And not only to the people in that era, or only the people of Israel, but eventually, *to all people. The joy of the birth of Christ is for everyone.* Maybe even if they don't know what we are, what we know, maybe even if they're not Christian, this should be the most joyous occasion, because it's joy to all people.

———

I testify that these things are true: Christ was born in the humblest of circumstances to Mary and her husband. This young couple was valiant in their faith, and He grew up to fulfill His destiny in saving us at His First Coming, and that He reigns over us now and will reign personally upon the earth in a day to come. That's what I always remember about Christmas, because that's what the angels said. "Unto you is born this day a Savior," Christ, the King, the Lord, and this will be a joy to all people. So it's my testimony that this is true, that He stands at the head of this Church today, and that through that Rock, His present Chief Apostle, He reveals our joy and our assignment to spread this with all. May we spread this joy to our family and all around us, and radiate it so everyone can see it.

———

Biographies
Gospel Scholars

Dr. Lili De Hoyos Anderson attended BYU and graduated in sociology. After almost 20 years of being a full-time homemaker, Dr. Anderson returned to school to complete a master's degree in social work at UNLV and a PhD in marriage, family, and human development at BYU, where she taught for several years in the School of Family Life. She is a licensed clinical social worker and has a full-time private practice in individual, marriage, and family counseling. The Andersons have eight children and thirty-six grandchildren (and counting).

Dr. Terry B. Ball was the Dean of Religious Education from 2006 to 2013 and is now a professor of religious education at BYU. He received his education from BYU: a BS in botany and education, a MA in ANES, and a PhD in archaeobotany with an emphasis in the ancient Near East. He has taught and traveled extensively in the Holy Land, including at the BYU Jerusalem Center. He and his wife, DeAnna, have six children.

Dr. Ross Baron was born and raised in Southern California. He joined the Church when he was eighteen and served a mission in Argentina. He is married to Kathleen Ann Bolton, and together they have nine children. Ross Baron received a bachelor's degree from BYU in finance, as well as a master's degree and a PhD from the University of Southern California (USC) in religion and social ethics. He was involved in business and entrepreneurship before he went to work as a full-time institute director and CES coordinator in Southern California at the Glendora and Claremont Institutes for the Church.

Dr. Daniel Belnap was born in Coeur d'Alene, ID, and raised in Pocatello, ID, and Sandy, UT. He holds a BA in international relations from BYU, an MA in ANES from BYU, and an MA and a PhD in northwest semitics from the University of Chicago. He is currently working as a professor of ancient scripture at BYU. He and his wife, Erin Pinney, have four children.

Dr. Lincoln Blumell received a BA with honors in classical and early Christian studies from the University of Calgary; an MA from the University of Calgary in religious studies (ancient Christianity); an MSt from Oxford (Christ Church) in Jewish studies; and a PhD from the University of Toronto in religious studies (early Christianity). Before coming to BYU, he held a visiting assistant professorship in the Department of Classical Studies at Tulane University in New Orleans.

Dr. Matthew L. Bowen was raised in Orem, UT, and graduated from BYU. He holds a PhD in Biblical studies from the Catholic University of America in Washington, D.C. and is currently an associate professor in religious education at BYU-Hawaii. He and his wife, the former Suzanne Blattberg, are the parents of three children.

Dr. Jeffrey R. Chadwick serves at the BYU Jerusalem Center as a professor of archaeology and ANES and as a religious education professor of Church history and Jewish studies (in the Department of Church History and Doctrine). At BYU and within the CES, his religious education teaching emphases include the Bible (Old and New Testament), the Book of Mormon, Church history and Christian history, Judaism, and Islam. Dr. Chadwick was born and raised in Ogden, UT, and graduated from the world-famous Ben Lomond High School. He and his wife, Kim, have six children and twelve grandchildren.

Dr. Jason Robert Combs is an assistant professor of ancient scripture at BYU. He joined the BYU faculty in 2016 after working as a lecturer at High Point University, Guilford College, and UNC-Greensboro. Combs earned his bachelor's degree in ANES from BYU. He holds master's degrees in biblical studies from Yale Divinity School and in classics from Columbia University. He earned his PhD in religious studies with an emphasis on the history of early Christianity from UNC-Chapel Hill.

Dr. Ryan Davis received a PhD in the Hebrew Bible and the ancient Near East from UT Austin in 2016. He specializes in the prayers and rituals of ancient Israel and Mesopotamia. Since 2015, he has been an adjunct instructor in the Department of Ancient Scripture at BYU, teaching at both the Provo campus and the BYU Salt Lake Center. His most recent publication was titled "The God of the Psalms and the Broken" published in _Old Testament Insights: The Sacrifice of a Broken Heart and Contrite Spirit._

Dr. *Jenet Erickson*, an associate professor in the Department of Church History and Doctrine in BYU Religious Education, teaches the Eternal Family course as well as Introduction to Family Process for the School of Family Life. Her research has focused on maternal and child well-being in the context of work and family life, as well as the distinct contributions of mothers and fathers in child development. She is a research fellow of both the Wheatley Institution and the Institute for Family Studies, and she has been a columnist on family issues for the Deseret News since 2013.

Dr. *Barbara Morgan Gardner* teaches religion at BYU. She is the author of *The Priesthood Power of Women in the Temple, Church, and Family*. Barbara received a master's degree in educational leadership and foundations with an emphasis in international education development and a PhD in instructional psychology. She served as institute director in Boston, which included her assignment as the chaplain at both Harvard and MIT. She continues to serve as the chaplain-at-large in higher education for the Church. She also serves on the BYU Interfaith Outreach Council. She resides in Highland, UT, with her husband, Dustin, and their two children.

Dr. *Michael Goodman* is the RSC's associate publications director. He has worked for the Church Educational System since 1989 and was the manager of CES college curriculum before joining the Department of Church History and Doctrine in 2007. He holds a bachelor's degree in journalism with a public relations, a master's degree in information technology, and a PhD in marriage, family, and human development. He is a co-investigator on the Family Foundations of Youth Development longitudinal research project. His research focuses on adolescent and family faith development and mental health outcomes with a special emphasis on suicidality. He has been married to Tiina Anita Goodman from Lahti, Finland, since 1985.

Dr. Matthew Grey is an associate professor of ancient scripture at BYU. He was born and raised in the Chicago area and attended BYU, where he received a BA in ANES. Later, he received an MA in archaeology and the history of antiquity from Andrews University, an MSt in Jewish studies from the University of Oxford, and a PhD in ancient Mediterranean religions from the University of North Carolina (UNC). Dr. Grey and his wife, Mary, have three children and live in Springville, UT.

Bruce C. Hafen grew up in St. George, UT. He received a bachelor's degree from BYU and a JD from the University of Utah. After practicing law in Salt Lake City, he went to BYU in 1971 as a member of the original faculty of the J. Reuben Clark Law School. He served as the president of BYU-Idaho, the dean of the J. Reuben Clark Law School, and later the provost at BYU. He was called as a full-time General Authority in 1996, serving in area presidencies in Australia, North America, and Europe. He is the author of several books on gospel topics, including the biography of Elder Neal A. Maxwell as well as books on marriage, the temple, and the Atonement — including *The Broken Heart* and *Covenant Hearts*.

Marie K. Hafen is a homemaker and a teacher. She has a master's degree in English from BYU and has taught Shakespeare, freshman writing, and Book of Mormon classes at BYU-Idaho, the University of Utah, and BYU. She was also on the Young Women General Board, the Board of Directors of the Deseret News, and was matron

of the St. George temple. She has edited and co-authored books with her husband, Bruce, including *The Contrite Spirit* and, most recently, *Faith Is Not Blind*. The Hafens have seven children and forty-six grandchildren.

Dr. John Hilton III was born in San Francisco and grew up in Seattle. He holds a bachelor's degree from BYU. He and his wife, Lani, have six children. They have lived in Boise, Boston, Miami, Mexico, Jerusalem, and China. John has a master's degree from Harvard and a PhD from BYU, both in education. John is a professor of religious education at BYU. John has published several books, including *Considering the Cross: How Calvary Connects Us with Christ* and *The Founder of Our Peace*. He is also the author of the video course and podcast *Seeking Jesus*.

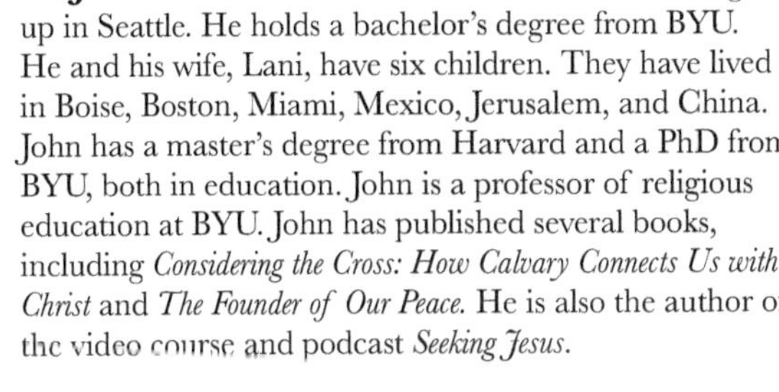

Dr. Shon Hopkin received a bachelor's degree and a master's degree from BYU in ANES with a focus on the Hebrew Bible. He received a PhD from the University of Texas at Austin (UT Austin) in Hebrew studies with a focus on medieval Hebrew, Arabic, and Spanish literature. He is one of the principal organizers of the ongoing Jewish and Latter-day Saint Academic Interfaith Dialogue project. He has authored, co-authored, and edited numerous books. He and his wife, Jennifer, have four children and two grandchildren.

Dr. Eric Huntsman was born in Albuquerque, NM, but was raised in upstate New York, western Pennsylvania, and Tennessee. In 1993, he married N. Elaine Scott. He received a BA in classical Greek and Latin from BYU in 1990, a MA in ancient history from University of Pennsylvania in 1992, and a PhD in ancient history from University of Pennsylvania in 1997. He joined the faculty at BYU full time in 1994 as an instructor of classics, becoming an assistant professor of classics and ancient history in 1997. He transferred to the College of Religious Education, becoming a full professor in 2015.

Dr. *Jennifer C. Lane* is a Neal A. Maxwell Research Associate at the Maxwell Institute for Religious Scholarship and a professor emerita at BYU-Hawaii. She received her PhD in religion with an emphasis in history of Christianity from Claremont Graduate University. She served as Dean of Religious Education and Associate Academic Vice President for Curriculum at BYU-Hawaii. She has published over twenty-five articles and book chapters on context and analysis of scripture, theology, and medieval studies, including her recent volume, *Finding Christ in the Covenant Path: Ancient Insights for Modern Life*.

Dr. *Jared Ludlow* has been teaching in the Ancient Scripture Department at BYU since 2006. He spent six years teaching religion and history at BYU-Hawaii and served the last two years as chair of the History Department. Jared received a bachelor's degree from BYU in ANES, a master's degree from UC Berkeley in Biblical Hebrew, and a PhD in Near Eastern religions from UC Berkeley and the Graduate Theological Union. He has published several books and has regularly presented papers at the Society of Biblical Literature meetings. He is married to Margaret (Nelson) and they have five children.

Dr. *Jan J. Martin* is an assistant professor of ancient scripture at BYU. She received master's degrees in exercise physiology and early modern history before earning a PhD from the University of York in sixteenth-century English Bible translation, with a focus on early English reformers. Before joining religious education at BYU, she taught for Seminaries and Institutes of Religion for

five years. Her research interests include early English translations of the Bible; early English reformers, such as William Tyndale, Miles Coverdale, and Jon Frith; the King James translation of the Bible; and the development of the language of English theology.

Dr. Joshua M. Matson received a BA with university honors from BYU in ANES, a MA in Biblical studies from Trinity Western University, and a PhD in religion from Florida State University. He completed his dissertation on the minor prophets in the late second temple. Josh was a researcher with the Scripta Qumranica Electronica project at the University of Haifa and an Orion Center for the Study of the Dead Sea Scrolls scholar at the Hebrew University in Jerusalem. Josh and his wife, the former Erin Barnes, have four children.

Michael McClean has been changing lives for over 25 years with tender songs and candid messages as a platinum recording artist. Michael McClean released his debut album in 1983 and now has more than 25 albums. He's directed some of the church's most beloved films, like *Together Forever, The Prodigal Son,* and *Mr. Kruger's Christmas.* He's written and directed countless musicals, including *The Forgotten Carols, Celebrating The Light,* and another more recent work, *Threads.*

Dr. Adam Miller is a professor of philosophy at Collin College in McKinney, TX. He earned a BA in comparative literature from BYU and a MA and PhD in philosophy from Villanova University. He is the author of eight books and serves as the current director of the Mormon Theology Seminar. He and his wife, Gwen, have three children.

Dr. Kerry Muhlestein is a professor of ancient scripture and Ancient Near Eastern Studies (ANES) at Brigham Young University (BYU). He has a BS in psychology with a minor in Hebrew (BYU), a MA in ANES (BYU), and a PhD in Egyptology (UCLA). He has taught history at UCLA, Cal Poly Pomona, and BYU-Hawaii, and he has been a visiting fellow at the University of Oxford. His podcast, *The Scriptures are Real*, addresses the intersection of faith and scholarship. He and his wife, Julianne, are the parents of six children.

Dr. Camille Fronk Olson is a professor emeritus, former department chair of Ancient Scripture at BYU, and former teacher at BYU's Jerusalem Center. She received a PhD in Middle Eastern studies, a master's degree in ANES, and a bachelor's degree in education. Her research focused on women in scripture, LDS/evangelical dialogue, LDS doctrine, and Palestinian families in the West Bank and Gaza Strip. She and her husband, Paul, have two children and four grandchildren.

Dr. Daniel C. Peterson received his PhD from UCLA. He is a professor emeritus of Islamic studies and Arabic at BYU, where he founded the university's Middle Eastern Texts Initiative. He has published and spoken extensively on both Islamic and Latter-day Saint subjects. Formerly chairman of the board of the Foundation for Ancient Research and Mormon Studies (FARMS) and an officer, editor, and author for its successor organization, the Neal A. Maxwell Institute for Religious Scholarship, his professional work as an Arabist focuses on the Qur'an and Islamic philosophical theology.

Dr. George Pierce was born in Okahumpka, FL, and received a BA in history from Clearwater Christian College, an MS in archaeological information systems the University of York, an MA in Biblical studies from Wheaton College, and a PhD in Near Eastern languages and cultures from UCLA. He is currently the lead architect and supervisor of the Geographic Information Systems team for the Tel Shimron Excavations in the Jezreel Valley, Israel. He and his wife, Dr. Krystal Pierce, have two children.

Dr. Krystal V. L. Pierce was born in Logan, UT, and was raised in Taylorsville, UT, but has also lived in California, Idaho, Egypt, and Israel. She received a PhD in Egyptian archaeology and Near Eastern languages and cultures from UCLA and a MA and BA in ANES from UC Berkeley. She has taught classes on Egyptology and ANES at the BYU Jerusalem Center, UCLA, and UC Berkeley. She has participated in archaeological excavations and surveys at sites in Egypt (El-Hibeh, E29H1, and Karanis) and Israel (Jaffa and Tel Shimron). She is currently the head registrar for the Tel Shimron Excavations in the Galilee region of Israel and chair of the Archaeology of Egypt session at The American Society of Overseas Research (ASOR). She and her husband, Professor George Pierce, have two children.

Dr. Dana M. Pike is a professor of ancient scripture and ANES at BYU. He earned a BS degree in anthropology/archaeology from BYU. He then earned a PhD in Hebrew Bible and ANES from the University of Pennsylvania. Pike taught for two years at the BYU Jerusalem Center and worked as one of the international editors of the Dead Sea Scrolls. He is currently serving as the chair of the Department of Ancient Scripture. He and his wife, Jane Allis-Pike, have three children and seven grandchildren.

Dr. Jennifer Brinkerhoff Platt earned a PhD from Arizona State University in educational psychology. She was a seminary and institute instructor for ten years prior to joining the religious education faculty at BYU and now teaches at BYU-Idaho. She is an author and a public speaker, having presented for BYU Women's Conference and BYU Education Week. She and her husband, Jed, met and married at the age of 41. They live in Rexburg, ID, with their two children.

Anthony Rivera Jr. holds a bachelor's degree in ANES from BYU and a master's of theological studies (MTS) in Hebrew scripture and interpretation from the Harvard Divinity School. He is completing his PhD at UCLA in Near Eastern languages and cultures. Dr. Rivera is currently an adjunct faculty of ancient scripture and religious studies at BYU. He also runs the HebrewBible.Info website. He grew up on his ancestral lands of Orange County, CA, and is a living Lamanite from the historic Acjachemen Nation in California and served as the Principal Chief of his nation and people. He and his wife, Jill, have three daughters.

Dr. Bruce Satterfield is a professor in the Department of Religious Studies at BYU-Idaho, where he teaches the Old and New Testament and Biblical Hebrew. Dr. Satterfield did his undergraduate and graduate work in the States and in the Middle East. He received degrees in anthropology, archaeology, and ANES. He has led many tours throughout Europe and the Middle East, and he also presents seminars on the Old and New Testament in Israel for tour groups. Dr. Satterfield taught seminary and institute in the Church Educational System for ten years and has been at BYU-Idaho for ten years. Dr. Satterfield and his wife, Carol, have five children.

Dr. Aaron Schade is a professor of ancient scripture at BYU and teaches courses on religion and ancient Near Eastern languages, history, and archaeology. Dr. Schade is the co-director of the Khirbat Ataruz Excavation in Ataruz, Jordan. He completed his graduate studies at the University of Toronto in Near and Middle Eastern Civilizations and is a faculty member at the BYU Jerusalem Center. His research interests and publications include ancient Northwest semitic inscriptions, archaeology, and the Old Testament.

Dr. Joshua Sears grew up in Southern California and served in the Chile Osorno mission. He received a BA in ANES from BYU, where he taught at the Missionary Training Center and volunteered as an EMT. He received an MA from The Ohio State University and a PhD in Hebrew Bible at UT Austin. He has presented at regional and national meetings of the Society of Biblical Literature, BYU Education Week, the Sidney B. Sperry Symposium, and the Leonardo Museum Conference on the Dead Sea Scrolls. He and his wife, Alice, live in Lindon, UT, with their five children.

Dr. Ariel Silver grew up in Northern Virginia and was an undergraduate at Smith College. At the University of Chicago, she received an MA in Biblical literature. She taught literature courses at the Waterford School for several years, then completed her PhD in English (American Literature) at Claremont Graduate University. She serves as president-elect of the Hawthorne Society and has presented and published on numerous nineteenth-century American authors. She is now an assistant professor of English at Southern Virginia University. She and her husband, Cannon, have one son and five daughters.

Dr. Andrew C. Skinner was a professor of ancient scripture at BYU when this was written. Born and raised in Colorado, he earned his BA in history from the University of Colorado. He then earned an MA from the Iliff School of Theology in Jewish studies and a ThM degree from Harvard in biblical Hebrew. He did graduate work at Hebrew University in Jerusalem. He earned a PhD from the University of Denver in Near Eastern and European history specializing in Judaism. He and his wife, Janet Corbridge, reside in Utah, and they are the parents of six children.

Dr. Gaye Strathearn is a professor in the Department of Ancient Scripture and in the ANES program at BYU. She has taught at BYU since 1995, including a year at BYU's Jerusalem Center. Dr. Strathearn has received a bachelor's of physiotherapy from the University of Queensland, a BA and MA in ANES from BYU, and a PhD in religion (New Testament) from the Claremont Graduate University. Her research centers primarily on New Testament topics, especially those of interest to Latter-day Saints.

Dr. Anthony R. Sweat received a BFA in painting and drawing from the University of Utah and a MEd and a PhD in curriculum and instruction from Utah State University. Before joining the religion faculty at BYU, he worked for thirteen years with Seminaries and Institutes of Religion. Dr. Sweat is the author of several books and articles related to the teachings of the Church of Jesus Christ of Latter-day Saints. His research centers on factors that influence effective religious education. As a practicing artist, his paintings center on previously underrepresented,

important aspects of Church history to promote visual learning. Anthony and his wife, Cindy, are the parents of seven children and live in Springville, UT.

Dr. S. Michael Wilcox received his PhD from the University of Colorado and taught for many years at the LDS Institute of Religion adjacent to the University of Utah. He has spoken to packed crowds at BYU Education Week and has hosted tours to the Holy Land and to Church history sites. He has written many articles and books, including *House of Glory, Sunset, 10 Great Souls I Want to Meet in Heaven,* and *Finding Hope.* He and his late wife, Laurie, are the parents of five children.

References

The Book of Mormon. 2000. Salt Lake City:
The Church of Jesus Christ of
Latter-day Saints.

—

King James Bible. (2008). Oxford University
Press. (Original work published 1769)

—

www.ingramcontent.com/pod-product-compliance
Lightning Source LLC
Chambersburg PA
CBHW060858140726
47996CB00001B/31

* 9 7 9 8 2 1 8 1 8 6 0 5 0 *